Common-Sense
Classroom Management

**for Special Education Teachers
Grades K-5**

Common-Sense
Classroom Management

**for Special Education Teachers
Grades K-5**

Jill A. Lindberg • Judith Walker-Wied • Kristin M. Forjan Beckwith

Skyhorse Publishing

Copyright © 2006 by Jill A. Lindberg, Judith Walker-Wied, and Kristin M. Forjan Beckwith
First Skyhorse Publishing edition 2014

Skyhorse Publishing books may be purchased in bulk at special discounts for sales promotion, corporate gifts, fund-raising, or educational purposes. Special editions can also be created to specifications. For details, contact the Special Sales Department, Skyhorse Publishing, 307 West 36th Street, 11th Floor, New York, NY 10018 or info@skyhorsepublishing.com.

Skyhorse® and Skyhorse Publishing® are registered trademarks of Skyhorse Publishing, Inc.®, a Delaware corporation.

Visit our website at www.skyhorsepublishing.com.

10 9 8 7 6 5 4 3 2 1

Library of Congress Cataloging-in-Publication Data is available on file.

Cover design by Michael Dubowe

Print ISBN: 978-1-62914-741-3
Ebook ISBN: 978-1-62914-907-3

Printed in China

■ Contents

■ Foreword

Special education is one of the most challenging areas in the field of teaching—and also brings some of the greatest rewards. The enormous challenge of ensuring a successful outcome for all students with disabilities is magnified by the need to individualize instruction. Teachers must work to be sure that these students have access to and success with the same curriculum offered to their counterparts in the general education classroom.

Special education teachers face all of the same day-to-day challenges as general education teachers. In addition, they must adapt and implement curriculum, provide behavioral supports, develop and carry out Individual Educational Programs, communicate regularly with families, and interact with multiple teachers and support staff throughout the school day. The demands on these special individuals known as teachers of students with disabilities are enormous.

No one knows the ins and outs of teaching better than seasoned teachers. No one provides more practical ideas and suggestions to add to a teacher's bag of tricks than a veteran classroom leader. Jill Lindberg, Judy Walker-Wied, and Kristin Beckwith share a history of many years of success teaching students with disabilities in an urban school setting. They have been selected over and over to serve as teacher leaders—Jill and Judy have mentored new special education teachers while Kristin has had considerable classroom experience.

Recognizing that every teaching situation is different—as unique as each child in the class—the authors present a clear, concise overview of the most important aspects of classroom preparation. They are the "don't forgets" for teachers. They are the organizational practices that keep the classroom moving in the right direction. They are the things that make all the difference.

Tips about planning, organizing, paperwork management, classroom discipline, behavioral supports, and working with fellow professionals and families are some of the essentials that can be found in this book. A teacher's week flies by in the blink of an eye—seemingly without a break—and these classroom organizational ideas provide the promise of a strong foundation of support for even the busiest and most demanding of times.

This book serves as both a starter guide to help a first-year teacher navigate through each challenge and an assist for even the most accomplished educator. It offers classroom management and organizational suggestions that hold the promise of a more rewarding teaching experience and of a successful outcome for students.

—Patricia A. Yahle
Director, Department of Special Services
Milwaukee Public Schools

■ Preface

Dear Teacher,

The field of special education is full of responsibilities, demands, and decisions, and as a new teacher (or a teacher new to the field), you may feel overwhelmed by all you have to do. This book was written to provide you with useful ideas and suggestions to help alleviate some of the stress you may feel as you meet these challenges. The new Individuals with Disabilities Education Improvement Act of 2004 (IDEA) and No Child Left Behind present additional demands on special education teachers. If you are seeking a text that provides help in teaching specific curricula, in demonstrating competence in core subject areas, or in obtaining certification, this is not the book for you. However, if you are prepared in the aforementioned areas and are looking for a teacher-friendly resource to use in your classroom—whether you teach alone or with a general education teacher—you've come to the right place.

The strategies and ideas you find here address some of the most urgent concerns you will face, such as special education instructional planning, general education curriculum planning, record keeping, behavior management, and family connections, to name just a few. We have taken care to make this book very user-friendly. Each strategy is limited to five points or fewer, and a lightbulb icon appears whenever the strategy has been adapted for younger students.

These ideas can be implemented without extensive interpretation or planning, creation of materials, or permission from your administrator. They cover many aspects of teaching students with special education needs and provide very specific and practical ideas.

We realize, of course, that schools vary from city to city and system to system and that districts implement special education laws in slightly different ways. However, we know that many needs and concerns are common to all teachers in this field, no matter where they are. We think you will recognize some of your own needs and concerns in this book. Keep in mind that these strategies can and should be changed or modified to fit your particular situation. They are not written in stone and should be seen only as a means to an end in assisting you in your ongoing efforts to provide your students with a quality education.

We believe this book will be a great resource whether you are a novice special education teacher, someone new to the field, a special education teacher trainer, or a mentor teacher. These clear, easy-to-implement strategies will assist you in meeting the many challenges you face daily and help to ensure ongoing success throughout the school year.

Good Luck!

Jill Lindberg
Judy Walker-Wied
Kristin Beckwith

■ Acknowledgments

We thank our colleague Jane Witkowski, who is an early childhood special educator at Doerfler Elementary School in Milwaukee, Wisconsin. She read each chapter with an eye to its appropriateness for younger students, and we very much appreciate her help and input.

We also would like to express our appreciation to Lisa Hansen, special education teacher at Allen Field Elementary School in Milwaukee, who read the manuscript. She contributed valuable suggestions and ideas that were incorporated into the book.

In addition, we would like to thank Dr. James Larson, professor and coordinator of the School Psychology Program at the University of Wisconsin-Whitewater, for allowing us to use information from his document titled, "Advanced Training in Functional Behavioral Assessment."

We thank the following reviewers for their contributions to this book:

Candice Hollingsead, Professor
Andrews University
Berrien Springs, MI

Darryl Williams, Principal
Gaithersburg High School
Gaithersburg, MD

■ About the Authors

Jill A. Lindberg has a BS in Exceptional Education from the University of Wisconsin-Milwaukee. She retired from Milwaukee Public Schools in June of 2003 and is currently a supervisor for the University of Wisconsin-Milwaukee/Milwaukee Public Schools Special Education Internship Program. Her teaching experience includes working for six years as a mentor teacher assisting both regular and special education teachers in Milwaukee Public Schools. She also taught students with specific learning disabilities for four years in a full inclusion setting and students with emotional/behavioral disabilities for five years, all in Milwaukee Public Schools. In addition, she spent four years in the Madison, Wisconsin, public school system teaching students with hearing impairment.

Jill coauthored *Common-Sense Classroom Management: Surviving September and Beyond in the Elementary Classroom* and *Common-Sense Classroom Management for Middle and High School Teachers* for Corwin Press as a result of her experiences with fledgling educators who struggled with classroom management. As a special education teacher, she wanted to write a book for new special educators and for veteran teachers new to the field.

Judith Walker-Wied is a Problem-Solving Facilitator for Milwaukee Public Schools working with teacher teams, administration, and parents focused on student achievement. She has worked with the school district for over 30 years. Her previous positions have included special education teacher for students with emotional behavioral disabilities and specific learning disabilities, diagnostic teacher working with the IEP team process, special education supervisor, and mentor teacher with the University of Wisconsin-Milwaukee/Milwaukee Public Schools Special Education Internship Program. She has taught classes at the university level, and she has also spent a summer teaching students with special needs in Southhampton, England.

Her educational background includes a BS in Exceptional Education from the University of Wisconsin-Milwaukee and an MS in Exceptional Education and Administrative Leadership, also from the University of Wisconsin-Milwaukee. The topic of her thesis was cooperative learning. She has recently earned her doctoral degree in Urban Education at the University of Wisconsin-Milwaukee, specializing in Exceptional Education with a focus on teacher mentoring. She has a profound conviction that student achievement can best be supported through teacher collaboration in Professional Learning Communities.

Kristin M. Forjan Beckwith attended the University of Wisconsin-Oshkosh, where she majored in special education with an emphasis on early childhood exceptional needs and learning disabilities. Two full years of classroom experience were included in her training, and she worked in various settings. These included classes for students with specific learning disabilities and cognitive disabilities as well as early childhood classes for children with special education needs. She also worked in regular education classrooms.

She taught in Milwaukee Public Schools for seven years, working with elementary students with specific learning disabilities and students with emotional behavioral disabilities. In 2002, she received a master's degree in curriculum and instruction with an emphasis in language arts.

1

Getting Organized

You are one of the lucky minority if you have a classroom of your own. Many special education teachers share a room, move from class to class, or even teach in the hallway. You need to be organized no matter what your situation, but especially if you are a traveling teacher. With the large amount of paperwork and other data for which special education teachers are responsible, having a system that makes sense and keeps important information at your fingertips is essential.

Chapter Outline

- Student Information
- Supplies and Materials
- Your Desk and Surrounding Area
- Forms and Schedules
- Room Arrangement

Student Information

Do you feel as though you need a secretary to keep yourself organized? Paperwork responsibilities can be overwhelming, and for that reason you need to find a system to help you keep current with your many duties. (Please note that IDEA 2004 states that short-term objectives in Individualized Education Programs can be eliminated for all but a small group of students who take alternate assessments based on alternate achievement standards. However, be sure to check with your school district to see if they plan to implement this directive.)

▶   1.   Your Individualized Education Programs (hereinafter referred to as IEPs) are the most important documents you will draft and refer to throughout the year. (These student academic and behavioral plans may have another similar title in your school district.) Keep them in a safe place that is easily accessible to you. You should have IEPs for all of your students on the first day of school. If you don't, inform your principal or the special education administrator in your school immediately. The IEP cover page provides a great deal of student and family data as well as the all-important IEP due dates. Make certain these dates are accurate, current, and in compliance with your district and state regulations or laws. Each IEP page must be complete, with page numbers indicated if your district requires them—and be sure all of the pages are there. Goals and objectives must be written based on your district standards. Double-check all IEPs for behavioral issues, transportation, and other supplementary services provided that are separate from the academic goals. If you have questions or feel you need assistance writing your IEPs, ask your special education supervisor or another member of the special administration staff in your building. IEPs are legal documents for which you are responsible. Be sure they are done correctly.

▶   2.   Having easy access to necessary student information is very important. Be sure you have names of family members or a guardian who has the legal right to make school and health care decisions for the child. Include current home address and home and work phone numbers and the times when the person can be reached at these numbers. Record the name of another person who can be called in case of emergency. In addition, know the correct last names of family members, as they may not be the same as the child's. You may also want to include the child's birth date, student ID number, or any other information that might be useful to you when having a phone conversation about the student with a support staff member or supervisor. Post this information near your desk or phone for easy reach. But be sure you respect confidentiality by using a folder or envelope as a cover. Put this material in a locked place when the school day is over.

▶   3.   Behavioral information regarding your students should of course be available to you in their IEP. Be sure you read and understand this data—especially if you are responsible for implementing a formal Behavior Intervention Plan. (See Chapter 7, Legal Issues, for more information.) Behavioral data may include a detailed explanation of what the child has responded to in the past and the type of incentive program that has helped the child to be successful. You may want to make copies of IEP behavior pages for yourself and any general education teachers or support staff involved with the student. If a formal Behavior Intervention Plan is in place, each staff member involved should have a copy or have access to one and should understand how the plan will be implemented. In addition, be sure you and any involved general education teachers and support staff are aware of serious behavior issues students may have in order to insure the safety of adults and other children in the classroom.

▶   4.   IEP snapshots are another way to have necessary student information at your fingertips and to share this important data with your general education colleagues in an easy-to-read format (Figure 1.1). Special education administration in your building or school district may have a form for you to use, you can create something of your own, or you can use the one provided here.

Figure 1.1 IEP Snapshot

IEP Snapshot for _____ **Special Ed. Teacher** _____ **Date** _____

Present Level of Performance in Academic IEP Goal Areas: *Behavior Goals/Formal Behavior Plan?* ☐ **Yes** ☐ **No**

Reading _____ _____

LA/Writing _____ _____

Math _____ _____

Other _____ _____

Supplementary Aids and Services Needed in Regular Education Setting? ☐ **Yes** ☐ **No**

Supplementary Aid or Service	Frequency/Amount	Location	Duration

Special Factors ☐ Behavior ☐ Limited English Proficiency ☐ Communication

Communication Needs _____

Comment on IEP Academic Goals Progress

Reading _____

_____

LA/Writing _____

_____

Math _____

_____

Other _____

*If applicable, please see attached Behavior Intervention Plan or other information re: behavior.

Source: Adapted from M. Nieves-Harris, M.S., 2004.

▶ 5.   Many students with a disability have varying degrees of medical needs, and both general and special education teachers must be aware of them. Share necessary information with the general education teacher, preferably in writing so there is no chance for error or misunderstanding. This cannot be stated too strongly. Your school should have on file any essential medical information such as the name of the child's doctor and who (including parent, guardian, and school staff) has permission to administer medication. You may want to make copies of these forms and have them in your classroom for reference. Some students receive medication at home rather than at school, and there may be times when, for whatever reason, they do not get it. You may want to keep a record of this so you can work with parents or guardians to be sure the medication schedule is followed. Often, school performance is affected by medication or lack thereof. In addition, take note of any side effects that may result from the medication. You will also want to keep on hand any information regarding therapy a student may be receiving outside of school if families have shared this with you and have given you permission to speak with the therapist. You can usually obtain permission forms for parents to sign from your school psychologist, social worker, or administrator. Some students with disabilities may have special classroom needs. Be sure you are aware of these and make arrangements to accommodate them. Finally, remember to respect the privacy of all of your students, particularly those with medical concerns.

Supplies and Materials

Sometimes it's a real challenge for special education teachers to obtain supplies. But part of your job is to be a strong advocate for your students' rights to the same education using the same materials as their counterparts in the general education classroom. Keep that in mind if you feel shy about asking for what you and your students need.

▶ 1.   As you begin to gather supplies and materials, make every effort to get copies of all the current textbooks, workbooks, and teacher's manuals you will need for your students. If you have students at different grade levels, then you will need materials for all the levels. Your administrator should be aware of your needs and supply you with these things. Realistically, however, this might not happen. You may need to borrow from your colleagues and even make copies of some of the materials. If you are lucky enough to obtain copies of books and workbooks that you use with your students, guard them with your life so you will have them for your own future use. Be sure to make yourself familiar with what will be taught from these texts in the general education classroom so that whether you teach students separately in small groups or within the classroom, your students with special education needs will always be as up to speed as possible. Be sure to check out the teacher's manuals as many of them offer suggestions for reteaching or even modifying work for students who need extra practice.

▶ 2.   In addition, seek out any other professionals in your building who can offer assistance with curriculum and teaching strategy information. In some districts, there are literacy and math specialists (they may be called something else in your school district) who can offer techniques and strategies as well as material you can use. This person may even be willing to come to your class or group to teach and demonstrate for you.

▶ 3. Special education teachers often use many different materials to support the learning of their students and are always on the lookout for places to find what they need. Teaching supply stores now offer many items that can be helpful, such as workbooks in all subject areas with ideas for adapting work for students with special education needs. Highlighting tape, word lists, and note-taking forms are just a few examples of other useful materials. Be sure to see what is available at these stores—and take a paper and pencil along to make some notes. You might be able to create some of these things on your own and save some money in the process. Be sure to keep a file of everything you purchase or create yourself because it will be useful through the years.

▶ 4. Consumable supplies are critical to any teacher's success, but they can sometimes become a huge problem for special education teachers. Often students with special education needs are taught outside of the general classroom setting. Asking these students to bring their own materials can be problematic. It usually works well to provide pencils, scissors, glue, crayons, and so on for them—and then have your students return these items when the lesson is over. This way, they will be available for the next time. Valuable time can be lost when students forget materials and have to return to class or to their desk to get them. Be sure you anticipate activities that require consumable supplies, and have them on hand and organized before your lesson. If you are scrambling for materials while your students wait, then you are the time waster.

▶ 5. Any effective behavior management system requires not only planning but also supplies. No matter what age you are teaching, you will probably use some type of consumable reward. If you know what grade levels you will be teaching in the fall, spend the summer hunting for bargains at drugstores, dollar stores, and garage sales. If you buy a little at a time, the strain on your wallet will be much less. It may even be possible to obtain free certificates for small edible items from fast food restaurants if you tell them you are a teacher. In addition, you may have a schoolwide incentive program where you teach. Try to incorporate this into your own reward program to stress the importance of following school rules at all times.

Your Desk and Surrounding Area

Is your desk a frightening and mysterious expanse that you are loathe to conquer? Do you fear you've ignored something very important lying on the bottom of the heaps of paper you haven't the courage to explore? An organized desk area is so important—read on for some valuable advice on how to accomplish this.

▶ 1. As special education teachers, we have a good deal of paperwork responsibility that goes beyond preparation for teaching. For this reason, finding a system to organize this information is very important. The use of baskets, totes, or other compact containers is one good way to do this. Consider designating a shelf for these receptacles or an area on your desk. If you put them on your desk, think about using stackable containers to avoid clutter and to ensure a workspace. Listed below are some ways to use your containers and to divide your paperwork so that you are better able to keep things up to date. You may think of other ways.

   a. Things to complete today—for example, IEP invitations, adaptations to assignments, letters home, and so forth
   b. Calls to make—for example, calls to the social worker, parents, psychologist, and so on
   c. Academic activities—for example, worksheets for current lessons for individual students or groups
   d. Daily behavior charts
   e. Ongoing paperwork—for example, IEPs, behavior plans, and behavior assessments
   f. Phone numbers—for example, student and family information and phone numbers, outside agency numbers, numbers for supervisors, and so on

▶ 2. Make your desk as functional as possible with classroom-necessary items at your fingertips. Your desktop should hold containers with paper clips, pencils and pens, and magic markers (with colors you often use). Also have available a stapler and staple remover. Find a small basket for scrap paper and sticky notes for writing and a Rolodex for important phone numbers. Keep additional pencils and pens, staples, tape, and other items in a top drawer that is handy for you. A calendar of some kind is another important item you should have on your desk. Write down all important dates including IEP meetings, conferences, report card deadlines, and so on for easy reference. Some teachers like a small daily desk calendar, while others prefer a large monthly calendar big enough to use as a desk pad. Whatever you prefer, don't omit this important item to help you keep abreast of daily, weekly, and monthly obligations. Remember that your desk or whatever space you have is off-limits to your students. Don't put anything there that could be a temptation to them.

▶ 3. Your desk should have a file drawer where you can keep folders for each of your students. This drawer should contain IEPs, cumulative folders, and other important information, and it should lock as it contains students' private information. If you don't have a file drawer, purchase a portable hanging file to use for this purpose. This can sit on or near your desk during the day and then be stored in a locked area at night. You may also want to make files for other important school-related information. These might include bulletins and communiqués from your principal or the office, items from your special education administrator or supervisor, school policy information, committee materials, and any other things you may want close at hand. If you work in various classrooms, you may also want to keep a folder for each one to hold things you need to know such as upcoming tests, special activities or trips, class schedules, or other information from the general education teacher.

▶ 4. It is important to keep your desk surface area as clean and organized as possible. A busy day often means a messy desk as there is usually little time to organize while you are teaching. But take a few minutes at the end of the day to clean up and put things where they belong. You may want to place things that you need to deal with the next day at the front of your desk. If you can manage to organize at the end of every day, you will feel more prepared when you come in the next morning. Remember that your clean desk can be a model for your students as it sends a message that the teacher is organized.

▶ 5. You say you don't have a desk? Discount stores usually have rolling carts or file-type drawers on wheels that can work very well and are not too expensive. Since they are usually one-time purchases, you can think of them as an investment in your career. They can be pushed to any area you call your own and will provide you with an organized way to carry your supplies and needed information with you.

Forms and Schedules

Teachers—especially special education teachers—are inundated with forms and schedules. Finding a way to make these user-friendly and useful is important. Here are some ideas.

▶ 1. Your students will participate in classes that are often referred to as "specials." These may include art, physical education, library, and computers/technology. Be sure to request a schedule from the instructors of each of these classes as your students must be included in all of them. It is important that you plan your time with your students around these classes unless it is necessary that you support a student in one of them. Also, ask all of the instructors what you can do to assist the students with special needs in working to their full potential in these special classes.

▶ 2. Refer to your IEPs to make certain you are servicing your students for the time period indicated for each goal area. Students may be serviced in a full or partial inclusion setting, or a resource setting where teachers work with individuals or small groups of students within or outside of the classroom. This will depend on the model in place in your school. Most teachers schedule blocks of time that are 30 minutes to one hour long to meet with a group. If you work with students outside the classroom, do your best to make sure you are teaching information that is aligned as closely as possible to what is being taught in the general education setting, so your students can keep up as much as possible. If you are supporting them within the general education classroom, make sure it's at a time when they can really benefit from your help. For example, if a student has an IEP goal in reading but not in math, you will want to be in the classroom during the reading period. Sometimes, it takes real thought to create a schedule that involves each of the students you service in his or her IEP goal areas—especially if you have students in many different classrooms. See Chapter 4, Grouping Students, for some helpful ideas.

▶ 3. To save time in your busy day, make forms and templates that can be reproduced and used again and again. Use lists that can be checked off or circled to save time instead of writing tedious notes over and over. Create forms for behavior charts, notes home, and meeting schedules. Using different-colored paper for different forms or academic areas is a good way to make it easier for you to quickly access what you need. Also, develop a form for your general education teachers to complete that provides you with information about what will be covered in their classrooms each week (Figure 1.2). You may also want to create something that will provide your fellow teachers with a schedule of days you will not be available to service students or when you will be involved in IEP meetings.

Figure 1.2   Regular Education Teacher Information

Regular Education Teacher Information

Teacher _____

Academic information for the following students _____
_____

Week of _____

Please use this check-off/jot-down form to indicate how best I can help the above students with their academic lessons.

READING

Pages to read _____

Seatwork during the week?   □ Yes   □ No   Day(s) _____

Homework during the week? □ Yes   □ No   Day(s) _____

Comments _____
_____

MATH

Assigned pages _____

Seatwork during the week?   □ Yes   □ No   Day(s) _____

Homework during the week? □ Yes   □ No   Day(s) _____

Comments _____
_____

LANGUAGE ARTS/WRITING

Assignments _____

Writing projects this week?   □ Yes   □ No   Day(s) _____

Homework during the week? □ Yes   □ No   Day(s) _____

Spelling words:

_____   _____   _____   _____

_____   _____   _____   _____

_____   _____   _____   _____

ADDITIONAL COMMENTS _____
_____

Thank you, your input is appreciated,

Special Education Teacher

Source: Jill Lindberg, 2004

Room Arrangement

If you are lucky enough to have a room—or even a corner to call your own—it is imperative that you make economical use of the area. Even if your space is limited, you must still service your students efficiently. So you need to be organized—here's how.

▶ 1. When setting up your room or your work area, it is important that materials and equipment are easily accessible with adequate space for maneuverability. Your chalkboard, dry-erase board, or overhead screen should be visible from all seating areas. You should have a table for small-group activities as well as some separate areas for those students who need privacy to complete their work. If you have computers, they should be separate but visible from all areas so that you can monitor students' activities there.

▶ 2. The materials on your shelves should be easily accessible and organized in a logical manner. Use totes, baskets, bins, and labels to maintain organization and to make cleanup quick and efficient. Make certain your shelves contain items such as manipulatives including chips, cubes, marbles, and so on. Also include calculators, rulers, paper, and pencils, or any other materials that you feel are appropriate for your classroom. These items can be inviting to some students in certain situations, so store them out of the way if possible.

▶ 3. Designate an area of your shelving to be used as a resource center, and include items such as encyclopedias, dictionaries, thesauruses, grammar guides, and specific topic-related materials depending on what your students are studying.

▶ 4. If you are traveling from room to room, staying organized is a special challenge. Using a rolling cart or file drawer on wheels that can be stocked with materials you need for each group can be a practical way to stay prepared (see this chapter under the heading, Your Desk and Surrounding Area). Keep supplies for different groups in separate boxes or bags so you can quickly transfer them to your cart—and off you go, prepared and organized for your next lesson.

Wall Displays

Are you wondering how you can put up a bulletin board display when you don't even have a bulletin board? If you haven't guessed by now, special education teachers need to be creative. Here are some suggestions that may work for you.

▶ 1. As previously noted, special education teachers often do not have much space to call their own. Still, it's important to be able to have a way to display student work and, if possible, informational posters to provide your group with helpful academic hints. Here's where you need to be creative to come up with something to use. If you work in general education classrooms, you might ask your coteacher if there is a bulletin board space or wall space in the room you could use to show student work and other teaching aids you may want to use.

▶ 2. If you are out in the hallway, use a tri-fold display board (sometimes used in science projects) that folds and is portable to exhibit student work and to show informational posters. You can buy sticky gum at drugstores or teaching supply stores to mount things temporarily on these boards. Since items can easily be attached and removed, you can carry your board from group to group and display different things for different lessons. Also, in the hallways, you may find cork strips along the walls for the purpose of hanging student artwork or academic projects. Use the strip to hang your students' work or tack up your tri-fold board with your displays already attached. It can easily be removed when your group lesson is over and moved to the next hall space if necessary. A tri-fold board can also be propped up on a desk or small table. So there really are a number of ways you can display student work and other teaching aids—even if you don't have a classroom of your own.

▶ 3. Now that you have some ideas about how to display things, here are some suggestions about what to show. Exhibiting students' work is a self-esteem boost—especially for children with special education needs. Be sure their work is prominently displayed during your school's open house, PTA meeting, conference time, or whenever families are in the building. Be sure to include items you have chosen as well as items students have selected. Informational posters that provide academic help should also be displayed for your students. These can include reading, writing, and math strategies as well as word lists, multiplication tables, addition tables, and so forth to help your students become independent workers.

2

Organizing Students

Staying organized can be a monumental task for many students, but for those with disabilities, it can be especially challenging. Teaching your students how to do this will save them—and you—time, frustration, and wasted energy. Knowing how to be organized is an important life skill, and your time will be well spent if you help your students learn to do this.

Chapter Outline

- Adequate Storage
- Teaching Time-Savers
- Student Desk Organization
- Mailboxes
- Routines and Rules
- Classroom Buddies

Adequate Storage

Do your students' desks become cluttered with paper and filled with unnecessary items? If you are afraid that whatever is put away will never be found again, consider the suggestions below to alleviate the problem.

▶ 1. With a number of different subjects, activities, and projects, students have many things to keep organized. Limit items in their desks to necessities such as writing tools and folders for each subject area. Use a different-colored folder for each subject with the subject and student's name written plainly on the front. Take time at the end of a lesson or activity to be sure each student has placed his or her work in the appropriate folder. If you are working in a space where students don't have desks, such as a hallway, consider a rolling cart that can be purchased at any of the large discount stores in your area. Use separate bins for each group. Then collect folders, writing tools, and so on at the end of the lesson, and place them in the bins. Over-the-chair-back sacks can also be found in some stores, and these provide another way to store items. They can then be taken along by the students if they need to travel from your space to their classroom and vice versa.

▶   2.   If you only have a small space to call your own, stackable crates can have many uses. They stack easily and safely and are compact enough to be used even in a hallway space. If you need to travel, find something with wheels. You might be able to find these crates or other storage containers such as small rolling files in your school. Let other teachers and your school engineer know what you need. These stackable crates can help you keep your students' materials and supplies—and your own as well—easily accessible to you and to them.

▶   3.   Be sure you've organized things in your bins or crates so you or your students can access them quickly. Older students should easily be able to find their materials themselves in your storage areas. Find a way to store textbooks separately so they don't take up space needed for students' materials. Use bookshelves if you have them, or bins, or even stack books on the floor if space is limited for you. For whatever reason, it may not be practical to make your students responsible for their textbooks, so make provisions to handle them yourself. Also consider small standing file containers with hanging folders that can fit on a desk and can be purchased at office supply stores. These can be useful for storing current student work or anything else to which you or your students need easy access. They are light and easily movable.

▶   4.   Remember that older students can help a great deal with distributing books, collecting papers, filing materials, and so forth. So don't burden yourself with jobs that can be given to them. Even if your classroom is the hallway, you can teach your students to help keep their space—and yours—organized.

▶   5.   Some of the things suggested in this strategy will require an initial monetary investment by you. Even though you may need to purchase them yourself, consider this a long-term investment as these items can be used throughout your teaching career. Most can be found at large discount stores, and they are frequently on sale—watch for bargains.

Teaching Time-Savers

Are you frustrated by the amount of time you spend getting yourself and your students ready for your lessons? Disorganization is a huge time-waster. If you feel this could be a problem for you and your students, here are some effective ways to handle it.

▶   1.   Many special education teachers have very limited space to call their own, which makes it important to keep materials organized and accessible. If you travel or are in a hallway classroom, this can be tied to the success of your lessons and ultimately, your students' academic success. If you constantly rummage and search for supplies while your students wait, learning time is wasted. If you keep your movable cart stocked with paper, pencils, and other necessary supplies, you and your students will be sure to have what is needed.

▶ 2. Sometimes students with disabilities have a difficult time keeping track of their things, and you can avoid arguing and excuses by passing out pencils, crayons, or scissors for a project. Then collect them at the end of class. You may not want to spend your own money to buy paper, notebooks, or folders, so have your students purchase these things. Then collect them, and dispense when needed. Keep textbooks and similar items yourself. Have a student distribute them and collect them again when they are no longer part of the lesson.

▶ 3. If you are working in a classroom situation where your students have their own desks, it's important to help them stay organized and clutter-free. Weekly desk cleaning can help—and desks need to pass your inspection when cleaning is done. This can actually be a time-saving activity as evidenced by easier access to material and supplies for your students as a result. As noted in the previous strategy, using color-coded folders for different academic subjects can be another real time-saver. In general, teaching your students how to organize themselves and their materials will allow them more learning time. Also, some students have organizational goals written into their IEPs that must be addressed.

▶ 4. Students sometimes bring non-school-related items to class. This can create a significant problem for several reasons. Some students with disabilities can be easily distracted and may focus on the object instead of your lesson. These things can also cause disputes, and you may not know to whom the item really belongs. If you have ever been involved in one of these squabbles, you know what a time-waster it can be. So eliminate this problem by setting some rules. For example, the first time a non-school-related item is brought, a warning will be given, and you will hold the item until the end of the day. The second time, either a family member must retrieve the item, or it will be held by you until the end of the school year.

▶ 5. "A place for everything, and everything in its place" is a good axiom to follow if you actually have a classroom of your own. Once again, if you and your materials are organized and easily accessible, you will have more of that valuable teaching time you are looking for. Small, daily cleanups and reorganizing can really help—then at the end of the week, do a major sweep of the classroom so everything is in place for the start of the next school week. You might even be able to entice some of your students to stay in during their lunch recess or after school to help. Keep in mind that if you are organized and well prepared, you are setting a good example for your students and are helping them to learn an important life skill.

Student Desk Organization

If you've read this chapter so far, you are probably wondering what more can be said about helping students to stay organized. But look at the following for some very specific ideas that will really help if you are in a situation where students have their own desks.

▶ 1. Show students how to place their materials inside their desks—folders on one side and notebooks on the other. Pencil, pens, markers, and erasers should have a designated place such as in a small pencil box, cup, or bag. You could even put these items in a basket in the middle of a group table. Weekly desk cleaning will help to keep the order you have helped your students create.

▶ 2. Repeat desk-organizing instructions on a daily basis at first and then once a week or so. It might be helpful to post these instructions in the classroom, and remind the students to read them. If someone is really struggling with organization, take a picture of how the desk should look, and tape it to the top of the student's desk—or create a large poster showing a well-organized desk as a reference for all students.

▶ 3. Another way to help your students with disabilities stay organized is to use the buddy system. Seat your student next to someone who can help with arranging the student's materials and desk. But be sure to find a way to pair these students so no one is embarrassed or insulted.

Mailboxes

Student mailboxes seem to be widely used and are a great way to disseminate student work and school information. Even if you don't have a classroom of your own, mailboxes can be a time-saving idea. Read on to see how.

▶ 1. Designating an area in the room to create mailboxes for your students can be a real time-saver for you. Use baskets, bins, cardboard shelving, or even shoe boxes to organize this area. If you decide on shoe boxes, ask each student to bring one from home—and an extra one if they are able to, in case someone forgets. Each student should have his or her own mailbox to be used to store homework, school information, and completed assignments.

▶ 2. Encourage students to check their mailboxes at the end of each day and transfer the contents into their book bags. Mailboxes can also be used to take home items from their desks that are creating clutter. Teach students to place homework in their mailboxes immediately upon receiving it to insure it will go home with them.

▶ 3. Mailboxes can also be very convenient for you. When a student is absent, you can place all assignments and school information that was distributed during the absence into the mailboxes of those students. Then you don't have to try to keep track of the things the student missed.

▶ 4. If you are a teacher who does not have a classroom of your own where you can provide mailboxes, there are other choices. If your students are in a general education classroom where there are mailboxes, take some time at the end of your day to go to the classroom(s) and deliver materials for your students. If no mailboxes are available, provide a pocket folder for each student where you can put materials that need to go home. One way to organize these folders is to label one side "leave home" and the other side "bring back." This helps students—and families—stay organized and avoid confusion. This can be especially helpful during the first weeks of school when many letters and forms go home—some of which may need to be signed and returned. Deliver these at the end of the school day so you can be sure your students won't lose them before they leave school.

▶ 5. Another thing that can be used as a mailbox is a shoe bag that can easily be hung in a convenient place—and even moved if you need to go to different classes where homework and other materials are gathered to send home with students. Removable numbers or names can be taped to each pocket that can easily be changed throughout the year if necessary and can be reused again the following year.

Routines and Rules

Most children need and want structure in their lives, which classroom routines and rules help provide. The key, however, is to be consistent in the use of them. Consider the suggestions below.

▶ 1. Routines and rules must be established and posted in your classroom to create consistency and an orderly environment. Establish your own routines based on scheduling and your teaching style, and follow them as much as possible so your students know what to expect. If you work only with small groups and your classroom is a hallway or other small space, this still applies. Post your rules on the back of an extra chair if that's all the space you have. Haphazard routines and inconsistency in following classroom or group rules can negatively affect your students' ability to learn.

▶ 2. Let your students help create your classroom or group rules as this will encourage them to take ownership. Decide on three to five of these rules. Be sure they are measurable and observable, and state them in the positive—for example, "Ask permission to leave your seat" rather than "Do not get out of your seat unless you ask the teacher." Classroom routines need to be practiced to be sure everyone understands the procedures. Lining up at the door, moving around the room for changes in activities, sharpening pencils, and walking in the hallway are just some of the classroom routines you may want to physically practice with your class or group. All children benefit from repetition, and it can be particularly helpful to students with special education needs.

▶ 3. Review your classroom or group rules daily until you are confident your students understand them—even if this takes a month or so at the start of the school year. Review the rules again periodically throughout the year to help insure ongoing appropriate behavior. Don't assume that one effort at the beginning of the year will last until June. Provide copies of your rules in contract form to be signed by each student—and send one copy home for family members to review, sign, and return. This will place even more emphasis on the importance of meeting your classroom or group behavior expectations.

▶ 4. Keep in mind the old adage that "the only thing for sure is that nothing is for sure." Schedule changes are sure to happen due to teacher absence, special programs, or other events. Try to give your students as much notice as possible about changes in their routine. It's a good idea to place a daily schedule on the board or another spot in your room or space that is easily seen. Review it briefly with students at the start of your day or the beginning of your group lessons. Some children with special education needs have difficulty with change, so if possible, don't keep them in the dark when a shift in schedule is in the offing.

▶ 5. Frequently, students with disabilities are involved in several different special education services and other activities throughout the week. Older students, perhaps fourth grade and above, should have a copy of their weekly schedule that includes resource time with the special education teacher, speech therapy, occupational therapy, piano lessons, and so forth. They should then be responsible for their own individual timetables and, in turn, take some of the pressure off you to do the coordinating.

Classroom Buddies

As a special education teacher, you have duties almost too numerous to count, and the most important one is to help assure the academic success of your students. If you don't have an adult teacher assistant, consider using classroom buddies as helpers.

▶ 1. Your own teaching situation will dictate whether you can make use of the buddy system to help your students with disabilities, and if so, how. If you are teaching in an inclusive classroom, it should be possible for you to identify students who would make good buddies. You will want to look for outgoing, friendly, reasonably mature children who are good students and who get along with others. If you are not in a fully or partially inclusive setting, you might still be able to use the buddy system with your students. Work with the general education teacher and have the teacher use this person if you aren't in the classroom to help your student(s) with disabilities. If you are in a resource setting or even in a self-contained classroom (a classroom where students with disabilities spend most of their school day), you may be able to work with a general education teacher to have some students come to your room—or space—to help as buddies for an agreed-upon period of time.

▶ 2. Some ways these buddy students could be helpful include assisting with desk organization, acting as reading or math buddies by helping their friend follow along and stay on task, and assisting in organizing homework and other items to go home at the end of the school day. You will be able to decide on tasks for your buddies based on your own students' needs.

▶ 3. You will want to talk with the buddy student and the person to whom the student is assigned to be sure they both understand the purpose of the pairing. Be honest but sensitive in discussing the reason(s) with them. Both students should understand that when they work together, it should not be a time for chatting or playing. In addition, be sure the buddy student understands that his or her job is to provide a helping hand and not to do the work for his or her friend. Establish a periodic check-in with the two students to be sure things are going as planned. You may want to inform the parents of the classroom buddies about this program. Assure them that all students involved will benefit and that no one will miss out on any classroom learning. You may even want to ask for the parents' feedback if their children talk about being a buddy or having a buddy.

▶ 4. If things are not working out well between the two students, don't be afraid to change partners and try to find a more compatible pairing. Don't waste too much time on this, however, if no one seems to be able to work well with a particular student with special needs. For a variety of reasons, your student may have difficulty relating to others, and he or she may do better under your direct supervision.

▶ 5. To encourage harmony and effort on the part of the students who are in your buddy program, you might want to consider an occasional reward, which could be provided in a variety of ways. You could plan individual or group rewards for the buddy students and give your pairs a special treat or even a time when they could be involved in a fun activity together. If you are concerned that other students may feel slighted because they aren't involved, make it clear that you are always looking for new buddies, and describe the characteristics of a person who could do this job. Then, if possible, change buddies occasionally to give this opportunity to other qualified students.

3

Classroom and Behavior Management

Special education teachers can tell you that managing behavior can be the single-most difficult part of the job. Some, but certainly not all, students with disabilities may exhibit negative behaviors that can cause continued disruptions in a classroom or group. Unless you are able to deal with them in a successful way, teaching and learning will be limited. The strategies in this chapter can help you handle some of the behaviors you may encounter.

Chapter Outline

- Whole-Class Management
- Considerations for Students With Special Education Needs
- Managing Small Groups
- Developing Appropriate and Easily Implemented Behavior Programs
- Developing and Monitoring Behavior Intervention Plans
- Incentive Programs
- Negative Consequences
- When You Must Discipline

Whole-Class Management

If you are in a general education classroom full time, you and your coteacher should work together to develop a classroom management system. If you are working in an inclusive classroom on a part-time basis, then you are in a classroom that "belongs" to another teacher. So the reality is that for the most part, you will need to follow that person's management system. If that system is effective, it will help to minimize problems; if it is not, you may need some help. Here are some good suggestions for either eventuality.

▶ 1. If you teach full time in a fully inclusive classroom, then you and your partner should truly be coteachers. All of the students should view both of you as their teachers. So one of the first things you need to do is to establish your credibility. Don't sit back and let the general education teacher take charge of everything that goes on—especially classroom management, including rewards and negative consequences. During your planning time together, be sure you are scheduled to teach some of the whole-group lessons. Then decide together what coteaching format you will use. There are several you can use, and some of them are listed below.

    a. One teacher teaches the whole-group lesson while the other circulates, observing classroom behavior and attention and assisting students if necessary.

    b. The class is divided into two groups, and one teacher teaches each group.

    c. One teacher works with a large group while the other works with a smaller group that may need more individualized help.

    d. Both teachers share the whole-group teaching of the lesson.

You may use all of these at different times. As you plan, however, consider the dynamics of your classroom, and decide which format(s) would maximize learning and minimize disruption.

▶ 2. Keep in mind, however, that you are still responsible for your students with special education needs. In an ideal situation, both you and the general education teacher should be accountable for all students in the classroom. But the reality often is that students with special education needs can sometimes present challenging behaviors and need more intensive support and direction—from you. If there is a solid classroom management system in place and a reward and negative consequence structure that works, managing challenging behaviors will be less difficult. So work with your teaching partner to be sure this is the case.

▶ 3. An important way to help your students with special needs succeed is to do some strategic classroom seating. If you have students who exhibit challenging behaviors, seat them in an area surrounded by those who have good self-control and a positive school attitude. If you have students who are functioning below grade level, sit them near buddies who are able and willing to provide some assistance occasionally. You may have a student who works better by him- or herself—someone who is easily distracted by others or who likes an audience for bad behavior. In this case, you may want to consider seating away from the group.

But make sure you have done enough observing and are confident that it would be in the best interest of the student for him or her to be separated somewhat from others. Then be sure to watch to see if there are positive behavior changes.

▶ 4. You and your coteacher should do your best to make sure that the students with special education needs are an integral part of the general education classroom. They should be fully involved in all classroom endeavors. Small-group activities should be planned with ability and gender diversity in mind. In order to ensure this happens for all of your students with disabilities, you may need to plan adaptations for seatwork or other assignments and create behavior management plans to enable them to be part of the class as a whole.

▶ 5. Your students with special education needs should understand the classroom rules and classroom routine and structure. It is your job to be sure this happens. In addition, you may need extra rules or additional structure specific to some of your students that will help them blend into the general education classroom dynamics. Social acceptance by peers and a feeling of belonging to the group can help increase the likelihood of appropriate behavior and academic success.

Considerations for Students With Special Education Needs

Many students with special education needs are now included to a great degree in general education classrooms. In order for them to succeed academically and behaviorally within that setting, they need support from you and from within the classroom from peers and the general education teacher. Here are ways to assure that happens.

▶ 1. The first and best way you can advocate for your students with special education needs is to develop a successful working relationship with their general education teacher(s). If you are in a full inclusion setting, work with the other person to develop a coteaching plan that will divide the responsibilities in a way that is agreeable to both of you. (See this chapter, Whole-Class Management.) Work to be a real force within the classroom—all students should view you as an equal partner with the general education teacher. Be willing to work with students in the general education classroom who could benefit from extra help. Call on the expertise of your teaching partner to help you make decisions about your students with special education needs. Go the extra mile when you can—it will pay off for your students and for you.

▶ 2. Whether you are in a general education classroom full time or part time, be sure students with disabilities are seated strategically to help assure their success. Work with the general education teacher to find them places among students who can help them occasionally with their lessons and set an example for appropriate behavior, if necessary.

▶ 3. Another important thing to remember is to help your students with disabilities to stay organized. Students who are prepared with materials and who have completed their assignments are less likely to create problems in the classroom or group. Whether you are in the classroom all day or only for special subjects, you need to be sure your students can keep track of their papers and projects. Devise a system—colored pocket folders for each subject; a homework sheet on which assignments can be written; regular desk cleaning; a container or pouch for pencils, erasers, and so forth. (See Chapter 2, Organizing Students, for more suggestions.) These are simple ideas, but they can be very effective ways to help students stay on track. Don't underestimate the importance of this. Time spent retrieving lost assignments, looking for a pencil, or rummaging in a desk or folder is learning time wasted. So use some of these ideas, or create some ways of your own to be sure you maximize learning time for your students.

▶ 4.   Work quickly to evaluate the behavior of your students. Seek advice and suggestions from the general education teacher and other support staff such as your school psychologist when planning behavior management systems for them. Your coteacher will feel more invested in the success of your students—and in you—if he or she is included. Review and revise these plans regularly, and refine or change them if necessary. Your efforts will help the entire classroom run more smoothly and will make you a hero in the eyes of your general education teaching partner. If you are in the classroom only part time, develop a system to monitor behavior such as a tracking sheet that can be easily completed by any staff involved with the student (Figure 3.1). Or you may want to use a contract in which the student agrees to a certain behavior in order to receive a reward (Figure 3.2). Older students may be able to use a self-monitoring system (Figure 3.3). Here a student observes his or her own behavior and records it. This helps students to be aware of, and to begin to take responsibility for, their own actions.

▶ 5.   Take major responsibility for working with family members of your students with special education needs. Dealing with some of these families can be challenging at times and may require the involvement of other support staff members. (See Chapter 9, Working With Support Staff.) Take the lead in involving these people if it is necessary to do so. But remember that if your student with special education needs is included in a general education classroom, he or she has two teachers. Be sure that family members know they can contact either or both of you if they have concerns or questions.

Managing Small Groups

Although working with students in small groups has many positives, it can also present its own set of challenges. Whether you hold your groups in the general classroom or in another area, the need for discipline, order, and cooperation are very important. There are several things to consider as you plan. Read on for some suggestions.

▶ 1.   Consider IEP goals and objectives as well as the ages and grade levels of your students as you organize your groups. Another thing to think about is behavior. Sometimes there are students who cannot get along with each other, and when they are grouped together, too much time is wasted disciplining. If you find this to be the case, don't expend weeks of learning time trying to deal with them

Figure 3.1   Monitoring My Behavior

Monitoring My Behavior

Student's Name _____

Date _____

My behavior contract says that I will _____

_____

_____

How am I doing this morning?

Great!	Good	Fair	Needs Improvement

How am I doing this afternoon?

Great!	Good	Fair	Needs Improvement

Source: Jill Lindberg, 2004

Figure 3.2   Improving My Behavior

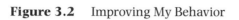

I need to improve my behavior in school this week.
Here are two things I will do.

1. _____

2. _____

If I can improve my behavior by doing these
two things, then I can

_____

_____

_____

reward

My teacher will help me by

_____

_____

_____

If I don't improve my behavior, then

_____

_____

_____

consequences

Student's Name _____

Date _____

Source: Jill Lindberg, 2004

Figure 3.3   Did I raise my hand to speak?

Did I raise my hand to speak?

Name _____

Date _____

Set your timer for _____ minutes when the _____ lesson begins. When the timer beeps, ask yourself, "Did I raise my hand to speak?" Mark "yes" or "no" on the chart below. Then set the timer for _____ minutes again. Continue to do all of this until the _____ lesson is over.

Did I raise my hand to speak?

	Yes	No
1.		
2.		
3.		
4.		
5.		
6.		
7.		
8.		
9.		
10.		
11.		
12.		
13.		
14.		
15.		
16.		
17.		
18.		
19.		
20.		
21.		
22.		
23.		
24.		
25.		

Source: Jill Lindberg, 2004

together. See what you can do to rearrange things. Perhaps the student can fit in another one of your groups, or you might be able to exchange students with another special education teacher just for this one subject. If there is no other option, develop individual behavior management plans for these students. Talk with them about one behavior you would like changed and what kind of tangible or edible reward they would like to earn. If you are diligent about implementing the plan, expecting compliance, and following through with rewards, you should see improvement. If poor behavior continues or escalates, you may need to develop a formal Behavior Intervention Plan. (See this chapter, Developing and Monitoring Behavior Intervention Plans and Chapter 7, Behavior Intervention Plans.)

▶ 2. Just because your group is small doesn't mean you don't need a management plan. Usually, you have a limited time to devote to your small groups, so every minute is precious. Some of the same concerns facing you in a classroom can become issues in your small groups. Seating arrangements can be important—have a strategic plan. Know your students, seat them in a way that promotes harmony, and don't hesitate to rearrange if and when it becomes necessary. Develop some simple, observable, and measurable rules such as the following: Stay in your seat, raise your hand to talk, and follow the teacher's directions. Use the rules to praise your students. For example, "I like the way LaTasha has raised her hand to talk." Create a reward system based on points earned for compliance with your group rules. Give small tangible or edible prizes at the end of an appointed time period for the accumulation of a predetermined number of points earned. This is a simple system connected to your rules that should be effective if used consistently.

▶ 3. As noted previously in this strategy, time is usually of the essence when teaching in small groups. Consider supplying materials such as pencils, erasers, crayons, and scissors for assignments or projects. You may be able to get some of these things from your school office; otherwise an initial investment at the beginning of the semester should supply your students with what they need. Look for back-to-school sales at the end of summer—you should be able to stock up on these items at a minimum of cost to you. (If you attend your local teachers' convention, you may find that a variety of useful free things such as pencils, erasers, and pens are given away.) Distribute what is needed at the beginning of your group, and collect the items at the end. This is a big time-saver. You may also want to provide folders to store assignments. Keep these yourself so that unfinished work is not lost. If some students seem to complete assignments faster than others, provide them with work from a folder of seatwork that reviews previously taught skills. Helping students to be prepared for their lessons and to stay involved encourages good behavior.

▶ 4. Finally, remember that you must do your best to see that your students have access to the general education curriculum during the lessons you teach. Try to find materials that coordinate with what is being taught in the general education curriculum. This will help your students to feel more connected to their peers in the general education classroom. (For more detailed information about how to do this, see Chapter 5, General Education Instructional Planning.) Also, talk with the general education teacher about including in your small group any students from the general education classroom who can benefit from more intensive help—your willingness to do this will be appreciated. Keeping all students involved in purposeful activities helps minimize problem behavior.

Developing Appropriate and Easily Implemented Behavior Programs

The main goal of every teacher should be academic progress for his or her students, but it will be a difficult one to reach if there are ongoing behavior concerns to contend with. So address problems before they escalate and become impediments to learning for all of your students. Look below for some ways to get started.

▶ 1. Early in the year, as you read through the IEPs of your students with special education needs, you will undoubtedly find that some have behavior goals. Usually, in order to address these goals, teachers must create individual or group behavior programs. Keep in mind that they need not be complex and should not be difficult to implement. These programs are informal and different from formal Behavior Intervention Plans that are addressed in this chapter under Developing and Monitoring Behavior Intervention Plans and in Chapter 7 under Legal Issues. Remember also that if you have classroom or group management systems in place that are used consistently and seem to work with the majority of students, you will have a context within which to develop programs for individual students that will have a good chance at success.

▶ 2. When thinking about individual students who may have behavior concerns, choose one or two of the most observable, measurable behaviors to address. For younger students, it may be best to pick only one. Be sure to decide on the one(s) that most affects the child's ability to function in school. Also, if you are able to change a behavior by altering something within the classroom or group setting yourself, do so. For example, if a student constantly disturbs or provokes his or her neighbors and, as a result, cannot stay focused, consider moving the student away from the group somewhat. If this helps, you have saved time and frustration on your part and helped the student without having to worry about developing a program to address the behavior. Then, if the same student also has difficulty remaining in his or her seat, you can address that—but you will have only one rather than two behaviors to deal with.

▶ 3. Consider talking with the student about the behaviors that concern you and also about the rewards he or she would like to earn. Setting up a program with no understanding of what might motivate the student to improve his or her behavior means you might be fighting a losing battle. Different things motivate different people. Find out, within reason, what might influence your student to work to change a behavior. Ask for some input and offer some of your ideas. Then consider having students work for points, stickers, stamps, and so forth for a specified amount of time, which will then make them eligible for a larger reward based on an array of things you both have chosen. These could include coupons good for such things as free time, computer time, special time or lunch with the teacher, classroom helper, and so on. If you want to offer tangible or edible rewards, the list is endless. Buy a large bag of popcorn, cookies, or pretzels, and let students have a small cup of one of these edibles as a reward at a time that is appropriate and agreeable to you. Discount stores offer many novelties for a dollar or less. There are also catalogues that sell small toys and other prizes at very affordable prices. Watch for sales at drugstores for toys, pencils, crayons, and other items.

Figure 3.4 We Know Our Group Rules

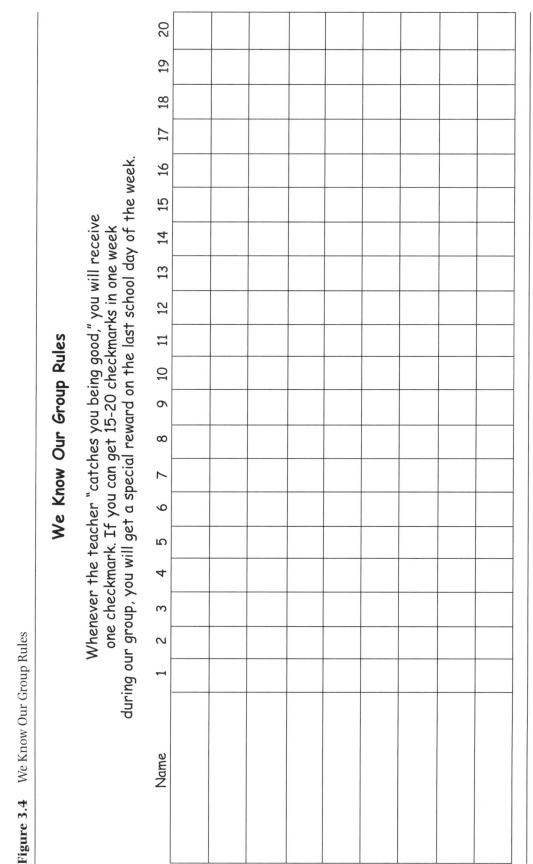

We Know Our Group Rules

Whenever the teacher "catches you being good," you will receive one checkmark. If you can get 15-20 checkmarks in one week during our group, you will get a special reward on the last school day of the week.

Name	1	2	3	4	5	6	7	8	9	10	11	12	13	14	15	16	17	18	19	20

Source: Sarah J. Schultz, M.E., 2000.

▶ 4. You can use the same format for a group reinforcement plan (Figure 3.4). But be sure to come up with some rules—you could include your students in developing these—that they must follow in order to earn points, stickers, stamps, and so on. Simple, observable, measurable rules are best—and ones that will enable you to control the group and teach. For example: Raise your hand to talk, keep your hands and feet to yourself, and follow the teacher's directions. The last one is a catch-all and covers whatever you are doing with your students at the time—things that can be observed and measured. Keep in mind that you need to connect the praise you give verbally and the stickers, stamps, or other items that you distribute with these specific rules so your students know why they are earning and how they can continue to do so.

▶ 5. If you have tried the suggestions in this strategy but continue to have difficulties with a student, there are a number of professionals in your school who should be willing partners with you in dealing with these students who have challenging academic or behavior problems. (See Chapter 9, Working With Support Staff.) But remember that in order to make a credible request for help, you need to provide evidence of a variety of efforts that you have made and have documented to change the child's behavior. Here are some things that should be included:

    a. Begin a daily anecdotal report on the child. It doesn't need to be anything long or involved. You may want to include information on how the rest of the class is affected by the behavior.

    b. Think about the positive reward systems you have in place in your classroom or group, and list them. Comment on how the student responds to them.

    c. List the individual reward systems you have created for the student. Comment on how the student responds to them.

    d. Document problems the student may be having in art, gym, music, or other special classes.

    e. Inform the child's family members, and keep them involved in your efforts. It is very important to make the family aware of the positive things the child does as well as the challenging behavior exhibited. Coordinate rewards between home and school. Don't forget to briefly document what you are doing to involve family.

At this point, you have given support staff members a body of information indicating that you have put forth real effort to change the student's behavior and that it is time for input from other school professionals. You may also need to consider a formal Behavior Intervention Plan at this point.

Developing and Monitoring Behavior Intervention Plans

The situation is very serious with one of your students, and a formal behavior plan is required. Don't let this assignment stress you out. Developing and implementing a realistic Behavior Intervention Plan really depends on common sense and a good understanding of your student. With these thoughts in mind, read on, and relax.

(The information in this section about Functional Behavior Assessments and Behavior Intervention Plans came from the Milwaukee Public Schools Web site, http://www .milwaukeepublicschools.org and from Dr. James Larson, University of Wisconsin-Whitewater. Please be sure you are aware of changes in the new IDEA 2004 that may affect you as a teacher by accessing your state and district Web sites.)

▶ 1.   School districts around the country develop their own formats for Functional Behavior Assessments (hereinafter referred to as FBAs) and Behavior Intervention Plans (hereinafter referred to as BIPs). For this reason, this strategy will not discuss specifics, but be sure you understand the details of how your district wants them done. That said, there are some general comments that can be helpful. Remember that an FBA and BIP must be done for students with special education needs who have ongoing or escalating challenging behavior or who have committed a serious offense. Be sure you know what infractions in your school district constitute a "serious offense." In addition, an FBA and BIP must be done for any student who has been out of school and has not had access to his or her Individualized Education Program as a result of misbehavior for more than 10 cumulative days in a school year. Check with your district to see what situations indicate that a student has been denied access to his or her educational program. Also see Chapter 7, Legal Issues, for more detailed information about FBAs and BIPs.

▶ 2.   An FBA must be done before a BIP can be developed and implemented. Data must be collected and analyzed to determine the target behavior. Some of the information needed could include how long the behavior has been occurring, interventions that have been used up to the current time, and progress or lack thereof as a result of using these interventions. Answering questions such as when, where, how often, how intense, what are the antecedents, and what happened right after the behavior occurs will also provide needed insight before developing the BIP. Again, be sure you know what kind of data your district requires for the FBA.

▶ 3.   Most districts have a form on which to develop the BIP. Look to see if it is included on your district's special education computer program, or ask your special education administrator. One of the most important things to remember is that the BIP is based on steps that staff members involved with the student will take to change the behavior, rather than things the student must do or stop doing. It can sometimes be a difficult shift in thinking to approach a plan for changing behavior this way, but the BIP must be written from this perspective.

▶ 4.   It goes without saying that more than one staff member will undoubtedly be involved in implementing the BIP, and it is not wise to develop it without input from them. As you think about the components of the plan and discuss it with your colleagues, the most important thing to remember is that the plan must be realistic. Don't create anything that either you or other staff involved cannot actually implement. Remember that if a behavior is so serious that there is a need for a BIP, then a workable plan must be created. Keep in mind that it is possible that the FBA and BIP could find their way into a courtroom.

▶ 5.   Again, each district has its own way of connecting the FBA and BIP to the IEP and making any needed changes in the BIP as time passes. Be sure you are clear about how these things are handled. But do remember that it is very possible the BIP may need to be revised along the way. It is your job to keep an eye on how things are going. Is the plan really working? Are all involved staff members implementing the plan? Is it difficult for some staff members to implement the plan? Is any progress being made? The plan will become useless if there is no monitoring and if changes are not made when needed.

Incentive Programs

You don't have to spend excessive time or money to come up with appealing and effective incentives—even for your most challenging students. Included in this strategy are things that are absolutely free to you and also things that just a few dollars will buy, as well as some ideas for simple reward programs.

▶ 1. One very important thing to remember is that your idea of a reward could be very different from that of your students. When possible, talk with them about things they would like to work for—within reason. Of course, you can't offer an expensive video game or a DVD as an incentive. So one way of allowing students to have a choice is to provide a menu of items that you are able to give as rewards. You may also want to have a graduated menu—that is, smaller items for smaller successes working up to grander rewards for successes over a longer period of time. So before you talk with your student(s), create a menu of things you can realistically provide.

▶ 2. You will probably find the need to create some individual behavior programs for certain students in addition to any group incentive programs you may have. Remember that simplicity should be the byword as you create these. If you design something that is too complex for you to implement or too confusing for your student to follow, it will probably fail. Often a student exhibits more than one inappropriate behavior, but trying to address all of them is usually unrealistic. If you are working with younger students who are kindergarten through second-grade age, decide on one behavior to address, and choose the one that is the most detrimental to that child's school success. For example, if he or she hits other children, talks out, and can't stay seated, clearly you will want to address the hitting first. With older children, you may be able to choose two behaviors. But even then, if a behavior program is new to the student, start with only one. You want the student to have success, and there is a better chance of this by starting with only one behavior. Below are two simple but effective behavior programs for individual students you may want to try.

   a. This one works for younger students in Grades K–2. Decide on a behavior to be addressed, and discuss it with your student. Be sure to state in the positive the action you want him or her to take. For example, if the student can't stay in his or her seat, don't say, "Don't get out of your seat." Instead, simply say, "Stay in your seat." This way, when you are connecting a reward to the action, you can say, "Tim, you will get a sticker because you stayed in your seat."

      i. You can buy small individual sticker charts at any school supply store or create them on a computer. Pick up some small stickers, too. They are usually not too expensive, and there are many included in a package. You will also need to offer your student a menu of rewards. These rewards need not be large or expensive—students at this age are usually satisfied to earn small items. Go to your local deep discount store—there are now stores that sell everything for a dollar. For about $10.00, you can get quite a variety of items to give as rewards. If things are boxed or packaged in large quantities like crayons, markers, and so forth, break up the packages and put several items in small plastic bags—there are zip-lock bags that are snack size and perfect for this. This way, you can stretch your purchases. The last thing you will need is a small clipboard. Go to your local office supply store where you can find a variety of sizes, and pick the smallest one. If you can find a large box to decorate and label as the prize box, then you will have something to hold all the tangibles and edibles you have—students love to pick out of the prize box. Then you are set to go.

ii. Set up your incentive system this way. Each day your student will get a new individual behavior chart clipped to the small clipboard. Write the target behavior on the top of the chart, and remind the student about the behavior you are expecting and the rewards he or she can earn. The student carries the clipboard around to each of his or her activities during the day—even special class teachers such as music, gym, or art should be involved—and receives a sticker if the student has acted appropriately. You decide how many stickers are required each day to earn a small prize out of the prize box. If the student has had a really good day, you might allow him or her to pick two items. You can manipulate the reward system any way you like. At the end of the day, be sure to talk with the student about why he or she did or did not earn their prize. Let family members know about this system, and send the individual behavior chart home daily. Write a positive comment on it when the student has done well so he or she can proudly show it to family members.

iii. Most younger students are happy with the daily reward they get and don't need anything bigger. If you want to give something more at the end of the week, give a large sticker—perhaps something with a positive word or phrase on it—or a colorful certificate. These are usually treasured by younger children.

iv. Remember that you want your student to succeed, so at first you may require a smaller number of stickers to earn a prize. As the student is able to perform the behavior more regularly, require him or her to earn more stickers to get a prize. Don't give up on this program. Track the progress of the student, and modify the program if necessary. Keep in mind that your student will have good and bad days. Don't give a reward if the student didn't earn it. Sometimes it seems easier to just give a reward rather than to put up with a tantrum if the student didn't earn it. If you allow this to happen, you will soon find that the student is in control of the behavior program rather than you.

b. Older students enjoy earning a variety of rewards—and don't dismiss stickers and certificates. Even fourth through sixth graders like them.

Inappropriate behaviors at any grade level can be serious, but sometimes older students' behavior can even be dangerous to themselves and others. (Please note: If you have students with special education needs who exhibit these dangerous behaviors, a formal Functional Behavior Assessment and Behavior Intervention Plan may be necessary. This strategy is not meant to address this kind of problem.) Below is one example of an informal behavior program you may want to try.

   i. A behavior contract is often a good way to involve students in improving their behavior (Figure 3.2). It involves the student in taking responsibility for him- or herself, which is a life lesson everyone needs to learn. You can create the contract with the student, having him or her help identify the behavior(s) that needs to be addressed. Keep in mind that you will want to choose only one or two behaviors, and be sure the action you want the student to take to improve is stated in a positive way and is observable and measurable. If a certain behavior is a consistent deterrent to school progress, address only that one. Usually the student and the teacher will sign the contract, and even a family member might be involved, depending on how it is written.

   ii. You don't need a fancy format for a behavior contract. Design one of your own to address whatever you want to accomplish with the student, and be sure to use a specific time frame, at the end of which the contract will be reviewed. Then an agreed-upon reward can be given if earned, or the contract can be renewed—and perhaps modified if necessary—so the student can continue trying. Remember that with elementary school students, you will need to limit the time the contract is in place before a reward is given. Begin with a week or less to encourage success, and use some daily indicator of success such as a sticker or stamp.

   iii. You will need to create a way to monitor the target behavior for whatever time frame you decide—hourly, half a day, daily, and so on. So you may want to use a small form that shows the progress with a check mark, sticker, or stamp (see Figure 3.1). The student can carry this form during the day so that any staff involved can provide input. Keep the contract handy, and be sure to review progress daily with the student.

   iv. Remember to talk with the student about what kind of reward he or she would like to earn. Of course, it must be within reason. Providing a menu of rewards may help a student who can't think of anything or whose own ideas are too grandiose.

   v. What about students who lose interest or don't want to participate? Make sure the behavior change you want can be achieved and is understood by the student. Don't set too high a goal, and don't wait too long to give a reward, if earned. You may find that the student may be more willing if you change one of these things. Another way to encourage participation is to involve another staff member besides yourself as a monitor of the contract. Perhaps the student has a special relationship with a staff member or looks up to someone in particular. Involving that person could be just the thing to influence the student to participate. Keep in mind that this person doesn't have to be a teacher. It could be someone from the kitchen, office, or maintenance staff. If the student chooses one of these people, don't hesitate to ask him or her. The individual may feel complimented to be involved.

▶ 3. Some students enjoy having time to do special activities as a reward. Below are listed suggestions that may appeal to some in your class or group. These rewards are meant to be earned over an extended period of good behavior—not something given after one good day. They can be earned as a group, and some can then be implemented individually or with just a few students at a time.

a. Lunch with the teacher is often a real incentive. It will be more personal if you have lunch with only one or two students at a time. Make it special—sit at a table in your room complete with tablecloth and centerpiece, or have a picnic outside in nice weather. Buy or bake some special cookies or bars for dessert. Make it a point not to discuss school-related topics. Instead, get to know your students on a personal level.

b. Special projects or outdoor fun can also be rewarding for students. Offer your students 15 minutes to a half hour at the end of a designated period of appropriate behavior to do an art activity or go outside to shoot baskets, jump rope, and so forth. Not an artist? Consult with the art teacher in your school—you might even be able to get needed supplies from that person. Or go to the public library where you will find shelves of books on simple projects your students can do. You can even offer a menu of activities they can choose from. The physical education teacher is the resource person for balls, jump ropes, hula hoops, and any other item you might want for outdoor time.

c. Many students' idea of leisure time is to watch TV or DVDs or play video games. Show them there are other options by offering a variety of leisure-time activities as a reward. Gather some simple table games, card games, and puzzles, and let students sit on the floor to play—even if your classroom is out in the hallway. Get some carpet samples—usually very inexpensive, and they can be used over and over—from a local carpet store for them to sit on. Doing activities in a more casual way, like sitting on the floor, can be a treat in itself.

d. Being a monitor for your group or class can also be rewarding. Think about things you need done on a regular basis such as distributing paper, books, or other supplies before your lesson and collecting them afterwards. Most students like to do these kinds of tasks, so incorporate them into your reward system. If your whole group decides on this as a reward, you can assign each student in the group to be the monitor for a different day if he or she earns it.

e. You may want to consider creating your own coupons so that students can choose their reward. These coupons can be for simple rewards that don't cost a lot of money, including some of those mentioned above as well as things like no-homework passes, sitting on a special chair that normally is reserved for the teacher, and being the teacher for a short lesson. You—and your students—may think of others.

Negative Consequences

No one likes to be the bad guy—particularly when dealing with students with special education needs who often have a number of obstacles to overcome. But understanding that there are negative consequences for inappropriate actions is a lesson everyone must learn, and we do a disservice to our students if we don't teach that lesson. Look below for some ways to do this with sensitivity.

▶ 1. "If you write on your desk again, you will be spending your recess in here with me cleaning desks!" It's a punishment that fits the crime and can be a useful deterrent to future scribbling. Developing a repertoire of responses to the mildly challenging behaviors of students with special education needs is a prerequisite for effective teaching. Below are some suggestions that are easy to implement as well as effective.

   a. Please note that the suggestions below are for mild disrupters—not those who are chronic and more severe. The ideas listed are usually useful with students who need occasional reminders and redirection. You may think of other strategies, but begin to develop a bank of things you can use regularly and effectively. If you are at a loss for a consequence or decide on one that is ineffective or, worse yet, punishes you as well as the student ("You'll stay in for recess for the rest of the month!"), you will be seen as someone who doesn't follow through. This could set you up as a target for some of your students with more challenging behaviors.

   b. Remember the "punishment that fits the crime" phrase when you decide on a consequence. There are instances where this may be a very strong deterrent to future infractions. Litterers and students who write in textbooks or on others' property are just two examples of situations where students can clean up their own mess and then do so on a broader scale. This can be a very effective consequence.

   c. What about students who talk out without raising their hands, are inattentive, or don't follow directions? First of all, be sure your entire class or group knows your expectations regarding these things. Include them in your rules. Before you begin a lesson, go over your expectations again. Compliment those who remember to follow your rules by saying something like, "I'm so glad to see Juan, Karla, and Tanesha raising their hands and following my directions to take out their math book," or whatever your expectation is at the moment. Try admonishing the offender with a compliment such as, "I'm so glad you know the answer, but please raise your hand." Then wait for the student to do so. If the negative behavior becomes chronic, you may want to create an individual reward system where the student gets credit of some type every time he or she remembers to meet your expectation.

   d. Chronic talkers or those who bother others can be very disruptive to a classroom or group. Separation from other students, however, should be a last resort. Perhaps there are one or two students who are able to ignore a talker. Place the offender between or alongside them. You might even be able to arrange a hand signal of some sort for the quiet students to use to remind the talker to be quiet. A finger to the lips would be an obvious choice. Sometimes just spacing students far enough apart can deter excessive noise. Seating a talker near your desk or near a spot where you frequently sit or stand can be helpful. Finally, instituting an individual reward system where credit is given when the student is quiet might work.

e. Inattentiveness can be very distracting to you as well as your class or group. Students who are digging in their desk, writing on something, or playing with a toy are not learning. First of all, be sure everyone knows your rules about paying attention. Also, you should already have rules in place about non-school-related materials. Take toys away immediately, to be returned and taken home at day's end. Be sure there are no extraneous materials on students' desks. Then, begin the lesson only when you have *everyone's* attention. If some are not watching or listening, stop. Compliment those who are ready to learn, and wait for the others to catch on—frequently, they do. If you need to stop in midlesson and wait for someone to focus, do so. Use proximity control, or make eye contact. If the student still offends, he or she may need to temporarily sit at a spot where there are no distractions, like a table or empty desk. Again, an individual reward system with credit earned for time the student is on task may be helpful.

▶ 2. Deciding on negative consequences that are sanctioned by your school administration and that are effective can be a challenging task. Empty threats teach students that you don't mean what you say, and after a while they pay little attention to them. Here are some things to consider as you decide on your negative consequences.

a. Don't choose something on which you may ultimately not be able to follow through. For example, if you have recess duty, need to make phone calls, and so forth, keeping a student in for recess for a whole month may not be practical. Before you decide on a punishment in the heat of anger, take a breath, and think about the ramifications of what you choose. You could have a student who fails to complete an assignment on a specific day remain indoors to finish it. If you are unable to supervise that student, you may be able to make a reciprocal arrangement with another teacher to do this on occasion.

b. Remember that constant threats to call home or even actually making calls when a student is misbehaving can sometimes backfire. If the parent is not at home or just doesn't answer, this will soon become an empty threat. Or you may reach the parent, but that person may be unable or unwilling to support you. Save parent contact for a serious situation or for something that has been ongoing or is escalating.

▶ 3. Talk to a peer about exchanging time-outs. You may be able to arrange to send a challenging student to spend time with another special education teacher—or even a general education teacher—for 15–20 minutes to cool down. (This can give you time to cool off, too.). You can return the favor when needed. Note that it doesn't necessarily need to be a teacher at the same grade level as yours. Sending a student to a higher or lower grade for a time-out may serve as an additional deterrent to future infractions.

▶ 4. What if your negative consequences don't work and a serious situation develops? Have a plan for a situation that begins to escalate to a serious level.

Develop the plan with teachers who have classrooms near yours, and have it approved by your administrator. Include some of the following things: Who will cover your classroom or group if you must escort a student out? Who could stay with a problem student while you escort the class or group out? How can you or a fellow teacher reach an administrator or someone in the office quickly? How soon can someone get to your area to help? Where is the nearest phone? Should you or someone else call 9-1-1 if warranted? As you plan, be sure to keep the safety of your entire class or group uppermost in your mind. Write down your procedures, and keep them in a convenient spot—don't rely on your memory when you may be flustered or upset. You will be much more able to stay calm and in charge if you have a crisis plan in place.

▶ 5. Remember that being an effective teacher and gaining the respect of the students is important. Your power to discipline students will be based on how they view you. Be visible in your school building. That is, know other students besides your own. Be sure they understand your behavior expectations in the hallway and lunchroom and on the playground, bus, and so forth, and follow through on them. Don't let misbehavior in these places slide past you—don't say, "That's not my student." Build a reputation in your school as someone who is fair but has high expectations for everyone in the building. Then, when you are asked to assist a colleague—whether it is with a time-out or in a crisis situation— chances are better that the student(s) involved will respond to you in an appropriate manner. Also, other teachers will recognize you as someone they can count on and will be more likely to support you in turn.

When You Must Discipline

Your method of disciplining a student can often have a direct effect on your success. Above all, remember that you are the adult and should stay in control of yourself—difficult as that can be at times. Look below for some other things to consider.

▶ 1. One of the most important things a teacher can remember when dealing with students who exhibit challenging behavior is to treat them with as much respect and dignity as possible. The reality is that often tempers flare and confrontations occur. But remember, you are the adult. Stay as calm as possible. Yelling or shouting is ineffective. If you feel too upset or angry, arrange a time when you can talk more rationally to the student. Often a problem need not be settled immediately. You may feel too flustered to make an appropriate decision about a reasonable consequence, so wait until you are calm and can think it through.

▶ 2. Accord the misbehaving student the courtesy of speaking quietly and calmly to him or her and, if possible, out of view of the rest of the class. A quiet and composed approach away from prying eyes may go a long way to calm a student and convince him or her to back away from inappropriate behavior.

▶ 3. Pick your battles. Is it worth a confrontation to make a student with challenging behavior pick up a piece of paper off the floor? Probably not. Is it necessary to stop that same student from repeatedly knocking things off another student's desk? Yes. Save face for yourself and the student by making a wise decision about potential confrontations.

▶ 4. Don't back a student into a corner in a discipline situation. Offer some choices to resolve the problem. This allows the student to see it as a way for him or her to make the decision rather than you, the teacher. Often, that's really what a confrontation is about—who has the power—and you've given some to the student in an appropriate way. Then, allow the student some down time. He or she may need a little time or space to cool off and reintegrate into the classroom without further embarrassment. These actions on your part can often deescalate a potentially serious situation. It's win–win for both you and the student.

▶ 5. Don't peg a student as a problem in your eyes and then make it obvious to others, because he or she will quickly gain a reputation in your class and even in your school—perhaps unfairly. Do your best to treat everyone alike. Even though you need to discipline or confront students with challenging behavior more often than others, try not to let those feelings color the rest of your interactions with him or her that day. That way you will send the message that you are unhappy with the *behavior,* not the student. Find something you genuinely like about that child, and concentrate your efforts on helping him or her develop that attribute. This may take time and patience, but it could help smooth the way for improved behavior. Also, consider that negative behaviors might be a student's way of looking for extra attention that he or she may not be getting at home. Spending a little one-on-one time alone with the student outside of class might help to improve behavior inside the classroom. Many teachers will allow students to come in before school or stay after school to help out in the classroom if the proper arrangements have been made ahead of time. This provides time to talk and get to know the student on a more personal level. It's a great way to develop a positive relationship with him or her.

4

Special Education Instructional Planning

One of the most important aspects of teaching for the special educator is instructional planning. Working with a number of students at a variety of skill levels can challenge even the most systematic and knowledgeable teacher. This chapter is aimed at helping you organize your lessons to address IEP goals and to maximize academic achievement for your students.

Chapter Outline

- The IEP and Planning
- Grouping Students
- Finding Appropriate Materials
- Independent Work
- The IEP and Assistive Technology
- Using Assistive Technology as a Learning Support

The IEP and Planning

A student's IEP is a legal document that must be addressed throughout the school year and should be kept foremost in your mind as you plan your lessons.

Academic programs for students with special education needs should be based on that student's IEP goals and objectives. Here are some tips on how to keep this important document in the forefront of your planning. (Please note that IDEA 2004 states that short-term objectives can be eliminated for all but a small group of students who take alternate assessments based on alternate achievement standards. However, be sure to check with your school district to see if they plan to implement this directive.)

(The information about Adequate Yearly Progress [AYP] in this section came from the National Association of School Psychologists. The Web address is http://nasponline.org. Please be sure you are aware of changes in the new IDEA 2004 legislation that your district will implement that can affect you as a teacher.)

▶ 1. Develop an IEP snapshot. This should be a simple form that contains the most important information on the IEP such as goals and objectives; testing information; and brief notes on behavior, present level of performance, and related services. Another thing that could be included in the IEP snapshot is space to include brief progress notes. Use the format in Figure 1.1, or create one of your own—but be sure to include this important information. If you work in an inclusive setting, be sure you give the general education teacher copies of the IEP snapshots for the students in his or her class because that person should be a partner with you in implementing the IEPs. Also, make copies of the IEP goal sheets for yourself and your general education partner. These things should help both of you work together for the benefit of your students.

▶ 2. Many special educators work with students having a wide range of abilities, and this can create a real challenge when trying to plan. Use the IEP snapshots to compare and group students who have similar goals. But be sure to look at the objectives, as they could vary from student to student. Several students of similar skill levels could have the same math goal but have very different objectives.

▶ 3. Whether your students are fully included or whether they work with you in small groups in or out of the classroom, consider developing a formal method of keeping track of progress made toward their IEP goals and objectives. Remember that for students with special education needs, your planning must be aimed at helping them meet these goals and objectives. Don't depend on your memory to keep track of each student's progress. Brief daily notes on cards or in a notebook are easy ways to document. You may think of other methods as well. With this information at your fingertips, you can do strategic planning for all of your students.

▶ 4. If you are teaching in a resource setting in small groups, you will have more control over your planning and your ability to directly address IEP goals and objectives. But if you are working with your students in an inclusive classroom setting, you will need to both teach and plan with the general education teacher. That person should be working in tandem with you to implement the IEP goals and objectives of the students with special education needs. But it will be up to you as the special education teacher to find a way to assure that this happens. Ask your teaching partner to meet with you as needed, but at least once a month, to review the IEP and make sure progress is being made on goals and objectives. Keeping abreast of your mutual students' growth will reap benefits for both of you at conference and report card time and also when you are preparing the student's annual IEP review.

▶ 5. Other important information that should relate directly to your students' IEPs is your district's learning targets or learning standards. They may be called something else in your school system. These are the objectives in each academic area toward which general classroom educators direct their teaching. So in order to be sure you are aligning your teaching as much as possible to the general education curriculum, be sure you have access to this important information. Be aware that a very significant impact for students with disabilities can be found in the graduated accountability measures that follow when students fail to meet AYP goals. If these students fail to make adequate yearly progress in reading and math, their schools could face a variety of corrective actions. So this accountability measure creates an even greater impetus than IDEA to link special education IEP goals to the content standards of the general education curriculum.

Grouping Students

Trying to group students in a homogeneous way can be like trying to use pieces of several different jigsaw puzzles to make one picture. If you feel overwhelmed by the variety of IEP goals, ages, skill levels, and behavior concerns of your students, read on for some helpful ways to find the right pieces to your puzzle.

▶ 1. Your particular teaching situation will dictate how best you can serve your students. If all of your students are in one inclusive classroom, it will clearly be easier for you to meet their needs. For most special education teachers, however, the situation is more complex. Students with special education needs are often placed in more than one general education classroom, and this means the special education teacher must schedule time in each room. If students are serviced in a resource setting (small groups that meet within or outside of the classroom), it can mean trying to coordinate your groups around several different classrooms' academic and special class schedules.

▶ 2. If you are working with your students in inclusive classrooms, arrange your schedule as much as possible to be in their rooms during subjects that address their IEP goals. You may find it difficult to get to everyone if you are working with students at the same grade level but in different classrooms. One way to handle this problem could be to arrange for students at the same grade and ability level and with the same IEP goals and objectives to come to one classroom for reading, math, and so on. If the general education teachers are in agreement and are teaching similar skills, this could work for you. Of course, you would be responsible for arranging the logistics of this and for implementing the lessons for your students.

▶ 3. If you work in a resource setting, you have a bit more latitude to group your students—depending, of course, on the schedules of the classrooms where your students are placed. One way to begin to decide how to group students is to use a grid format and start by recording all of the daily activities that don't change for each classroom such as lunch; recess; and special classes such as gym, art, and music. This will give you a very good visual of the times available for you to combine and schedule your students. You can then try to work around these activities to organize your groups.

▶ 4. Remember that if you work in a resource setting, your planning should consider two important things: the IEP goals and objectives of your students and what is being taught in the general education classroom. Even though the ability level of your students may be lower than their grade level, your lessons should reflect an effort to connect with the general education curriculum. For example, if students in the general education classroom are reading about insects, find some books on this topic at the ability level of your students for the basis of your lesson. If the math lesson in the general education classroom is about multiplication, use an addition lesson to teach beginning multiplication by using visual examples to show that 5+5 is the same as 2×5. And don't forget the documentation you are keeping to show the progress your students are making on their IEP goals and objectives.

▶ 5. If you are new, don't hesitate to ask for help from your more seasoned colleagues—most will be glad to offer you some useful suggestions on how to arrange your schedule. And keep in mind that it may be a work in progress at the beginning. You may need to make changes, or your general education counterparts may need to adjust things, so go with the flow—especially at the beginning of the school year. But as the year progresses, do your best to stick to the schedule you have created, as constant changes are confusing to your students and can exasperate your general education partner. Finally, remember to give a copy of your schedule to all the teachers and support staff with whom you work. Your administrator may want a copy also. If your students are in fourth grade or above, consider giving them their own copies of their scheduled time with you. At that age, students should be taking some responsibility for their school day.

Finding Appropriate Materials

Finding and selecting teaching materials can sometimes be a frustrating task for special education teachers who may need to scramble for leftover textbooks and other resources. Keep in mind that you are the advocate for your students with special education needs, and they have the same right to access the general education curriculum and materials as their counterparts in general education. Look below for some ways to be sure your students have what they need.

▶ 1. If you are new in your school and have few materials or none at all, do some investigating to find out how you can get the general education curriculum materials you need. Some schools have storage rooms where extra books are kept; other teachers may have extra copies of texts and teacher's manuals; some schools have math or reading support persons or other staff who often know how to access these materials. Certain school districts have centers that loan out a variety of curriculum materials to teachers much as a library would. Find out what applies to your situation. But if none of these do, you may need to go to your principal or the special education administrator in your building. Remember that you are not asking for yourself, but rather are advocating for your students who are entitled to the same learning experiences as their counterparts in general education.

▶ 2. Whether you are working in an inclusive classroom or a resource setting, you will most likely need to do some lesson adapting for your students. Some of them may only need accommodations—small changes that will help your students get the same results as the students in general education. But for many of them, you will have to modify work to their skill level or provide alternative materials. Students who are reading considerably below grade level will need alternative reading materials, and there are many good resources for these types of books. (See number 5 in this strategy for a list of Web sites of publishers who provide these kinds of materials.) Again, do some investigating to see if your school has some of these things. The librarian might know, or other special education teachers could have these materials.

▶ 3. Veteran general and special education teachers are good resources for materials. Find those friendly, welcoming people—there are always some in every school—and ask if they have ideas or materials they would be willing to share with you. But remember that if you borrow something, be sure to return it—and in the same good condition as you received it. Then reciprocate when you can, and offer your colleagues an idea or lend them some materials that might be useful. Another key person could be the school librarian. Tell him or her what you are looking for—that person might even be willing to purchase resource materials for you if the library budget permits.

▶ 4. Remember that as you plan your lessons using modified materials—high-interest/low-skill-level books, or other appropriate resources—you should be coordinating your lessons with what is being taught in the general education classroom. (See the Grouping Students strategy in this chapter for examples.) Do your best to work with the general education teacher so you know what materials he or she is using and whether you can access them for your students if you feel it is appropriate. That said, the reality is that it may not always be possible to make this connection, but do so whenever you can.

▶ 5. Another good resource for materials for students with special education needs is, of course, teaching supply stores—and you don't always have to bring your wallet. If you have a little time and paper and pencil, you can browse around, and jot down ideas that you find in books. You can also look for academic-related posters that might work for your students, record what you see, and make your own. There are even some academic games that can provide ideas for you. In addition, catalogues can be a source for ideas about curriculum and supplementary materials. Check your school library or the faculty room or other designated area for this type of information. Sometimes teachers have catalogues they use frequently that they can recommend or lend to you. Before getting out your own checkbook or credit card to pay for these materials, however, check with your administrator to see if funds are available as some of these books and other resources can be costly. Look online to find publishers who offer high-interest/low-skill-level books. Below is a list of some of their Web sites.

http://www.donjohnston.com Provides intervention materials in reading, word study, early literacy, and more

http://www.capstonepress.com Easy-to-read, photo-illustrated nonfiction books for reluctant readers in grades K–8

http://www.academictherapy.com Publishes High Noon books, which are high interest/low reading level

http://www.wieser-ed.com Books for students functioning below grade level, Grades 3 and up

http://www.perfectionlearning.com High-interest narrative and nonfiction books for below-grade-level readers

Independent Work

Another important thing you should prepare in addition to your lessons is independent work for your students. There will be times during the school day when some of them will need to be gainfully occupied with work that addresses their IEP goals and objectives while you work with other students. Don't minimize the value of independent work, but make sure that it is meaningful. Here are some ideas to consider.

▶   1.   The first things to bear in mind as you think about preparing independent work are your students' IEP goals and objectives. Independent work should not simply be busy work. It should have a purpose—most likely a review of skills previously taught. The work should be something your students can do by themselves for the most part. And there are a number of ways you can organize this kind of activity and present it to your students (see number 3 below).

▶   2.   You can, of course, create your own worksheets that specifically target IEP goals and objectives on which your students are working. Keep in mind, however, that teaching supply stores are carrying an increasing number of materials to be used for students with special education needs. Even though it may cost you money initially, the books will be useful for many years and with many students. So, you may decide to use some of both—teacher-made and store-bought materials. If you create your own, be sure to file away copies for future use.

▶   3.   There are several ways you can assign independent work, depending on the ages and skill levels of the students with whom you are working. For younger students, you may decide to have a folder for each student in which you keep both new and completed work. You can then decide on the type and amount of new work you will assign. This file also provides you with evidence of skill mastery or of skills that need review or perhaps reteaching. Remember, however, that students should get credit and be recognized in some way for completing this work. If you fail to do so, the work will be meaningless, and your students will have little interest in finishing it.

▶   4.   For older students, you might decide to prepare a packet of activities for a specified period of time such as a week. The students can then work at their own pace to complete it. You should, however, check in with them often during the specified time period to be sure things are moving along. You may find that a week is too long or that you need to provide more activities. For some students, you may be able to include one or two assignments that are more challenging. Remember, though, that independent work means just that—it should be at the students' independent level. They should be able to complete it on their own with almost no help from you. And again, don't forget to give credit or recognition of some kind for accurate completion of the work, or you will find it becomes purposeless to your students.

▶ 5. If you have prepared work that is aimed at IEP goals and objectives, and you are crediting and recognizing completed work, then independent work should be valuable for both you and your students. Another important thing to remember is that your students should be able to read and follow the directions on each worksheet; otherwise it ceases to be an independent activity for them and creates more work for you. So you may want to assign exercises that are self-explanatory or that are similar to work that they have previously done. Math calculation problems or word problems are self-explanatory. Sentences with blank spaces to be filled by vocabulary from a word bank is an example of a format that would be familiar and can be repeated. If your student will be doing some of his or her independent work in a general education classroom, consider finding a buddy for that person who can help with directions if necessary. By doing this, it will free you to continue working with others.

If you are working with very young students, independent paper-and-pencil tasks may not be an option. These students often require assistance and supervision with all activities, especially at the beginning of the school year. However, if you take the time to establish a consistent routine early on, many students in an early childhood classroom can become somewhat independent with activities such as puzzles, file folder games, and other fine-motor activities for short periods of time (10 to 15 minutes) during the day.

The IEP and Assistive Technology

The use of assistive technology within the IEP can sometimes be confusing for teachers. But keep in mind that this issue must be addressed for students who need it to demonstrate academic understanding. Most schools have a variety of personnel who can assist you with deciding how to include assistive technology appropriately in the IEP. For help with this and other questions, look below.

(This information came from the State of Wisconsin Department of Public Instruction Web site, http://www.dpi.state.wi.us and from the Milwaukee Public School Web site, http://www.milwaukeepublicschools.org. Access Web sites for your own state and school district for information specific to you and your situation.)

▶ 1. The IDEA legislation defines assistive technology as both a device and a service. The term *assistive technology device* means any equipment—whether it is sold commercially or it is something modified or customized—that will increase, maintain, or improve the skills of students with special education needs. The term *assistive technology service* means any service that directly assists a child with a disability in the selection, acquisition, or use of an assistive technology device. Assistive technology supports for students with special needs are available in many areas including writing, reading, math, study skills, communication, positioning and mobility, hearing, vision, and recreation and leisure.

▶ 2. Most IEPs must address the need for assistive technology devices or services for the student. Be sure you are aware of exactly how your school district interprets this. There may be a difference between the need for a device or service to benefit the student and the need for the device or service to enable the student to demonstrate knowledge. Some school districts make this differentiation and will provide the device or service only to enable the student to demonstrate knowledge. If you have any questions about this, be sure to check with the special education administrator in your building.

▶ 3. Assistive technology is usually included on each goal page of the IEP, and there will also be an area to address accommodations and modifications. Be aware that these two areas may overlap and can include such things as computers, note-taking devices, software, large-print books, taped materials, and so on. The overlap can sometimes be unclear. Again, be sure to consult with the special education administration if you are confused as to where a certain device or service should be addressed.

▶ 4. Be sure to check with the special education administrator in your building before you indicate any specific type of assistive technology, such as the brand name of any piece of equipment. If you specify a brand name, be aware that any school the student might attend must purchase that specific piece of apparatus— and it could be very costly. Using a generic term such as "talking word processor" rather than a brand name gives the school more choices as to what they will use to service the student. No one wants to deny students with special education needs the access to appropriate assistive technology, but budget constraints exist in almost every school system and must be considered.

▶ 5. Know the people in your building who can be resources for help in the area of assistive technology. They can include the speech and language therapist, the physical and occupational therapist, and your school's general technology person—this person may deal mainly with computers but could be an excellent resource for software programs that could be very beneficial for students with special needs. Also, most school districts have technology personnel who often provide workshops to help keep teachers up to date on the latest resources. Often, a districtwide technology department will send out newsletters that may include, among other things, information about these workshops. Find out how you can access this, and take advantage of what this department has to offer.

Using Assistive Technology as a Learning Support

Some of us are intimidated by technology and the speed at which things are changing in this area. However, we not only owe it to our students to keep up with the many new devices that are available to help them learn, but we also are mandated by the IEP to provide these services when required. So plunge in, and learn about these wonderful learning aids.

▶ 1. Assistive technology can be helpful to a broad range of students, not just those who have severe physical or cognitive disabilities. It is a means for students with varying levels of ability to access the curriculum and to aid in independent learning. So, as you assess your students with special education needs, think about how some of these resources might be used.

▶ 2. Keep in mind that there are both low-level and high-level technology options. Something as simple as a pencil grip for a student who needs to work on letter-formation skills can be considered low-level technology. Clearly this kind is less intricate and less costly, and requires little or no training. Other low-level technology devices could include such things as highlighters for text, large-print books, special paper, book holders, and picture-word communication boards. As noted in the previous strategy, the line between low-level technology and accommodations or modifications can be blurry. So, if you need to include any of these things in an IEP and are unsure of how to document, check with someone from the special education administration in your school.

▶ 3. High-level technology can be more complex and may require training to use. As noted in the previous strategy, most school districts have technology departments that offer workshops on how to use these high-tech devices. Some of these departments might also lend out these kinds of things to schools for a specified period of time. This can give teachers an opportunity to try the device with the student to see if it will help him or her to show academic understanding without having to purchase the technology. Be sure to investigate what your district's assistive technology department has to offer, and take full advantage of any opportunities.

▶ 4. As noted previously, the speech and language therapist and the occupational and physical therapist are also good resources for ideas regarding technology devices or services. Don't hesitate to ask for their help and suggestions. Since they are right on the premises, they might be willing to come into your classroom and help you assess a student, offer some technology ideas, and even show you how to implement the technology.

5

General Education Instructional Planning

S tudents with special education needs have the right to access the general education curriculum. It's your job as the special education teacher to provide that access—with your general education teacher partner. In other words, it's a team effort. This chapter covers ideas and suggestions that can help you facilitate this.

Chapter Outline

- Coordinating Efforts With the General Education Teacher and Support Staff
- Planning for Academic and Behavioral Success
- Coteaching and Coplanning
- Adapting Lessons
- Accessing the General Education Curriculum
- Transition Times
- Special Education Instructional Planning
- Your Involvement in the General Education Classroom

Coordinating Efforts With the General Education Teacher and Support Staff

Sole responsibility for the education of students with disabilities does not rest with the special education teacher alone. General education teachers must be real partners in implementing the Individualized Education Program (IEP) for these students in their classrooms. Often, however, it is up to the special education teacher to help his or her colleagues to understand their responsibilities. Read on for some suggestions as to how you can do this. (Please note that IDEA 2004 states that short-term objectives can be eliminated for all but a small group of students who take alternate assessments based on alternate achievement standards. However, be sure to check with your school district to see if they plan to implement this directive.)

(The information about Individualized Education Programs came from Wrightslaw. The Web site is http://www.wrightslaw.com. Please be sure you are aware of changes in the new IDEA 2004 that may affect you as a teacher by accessing your state and district Web sites.)

▶ 1. Students will learn most effectively if special education teachers and general education teachers collaborate. The IDEA 2004 legislation mandates that children with special needs are entitled to access the general curriculum unless their disability dictates removal from it. The IEP team will make this determination and justification. Both special and general education teachers are important members of this team.

▶ 2. There are legal responsibilities for the special education teacher concerning the IEP for each child with special needs. It is the responsibility of the special education teacher to make the IEP accessible to general education teachers and other service providers such as the speech and language pathologist, physical therapist, and any others who work with the child. General education teachers must be aware of their designated responsibilities for implementing the child's IEP and any accommodations, modifications, and supports that must be provided. As the special education teacher, it's usually your responsibility to make accommodations or modifications for students with special education needs in the general education classroom.

▶ 3. The IEP goal pages and the objectives on those pages will identify specific areas of need for the child that will help him or her participate in the general curriculum, as well as identify any accommodations or modifications needed in these areas. Common academic areas addressed in the IEP are math, reading, and written language. Be sure that the general education teacher and other service providers have a copy of the IEP—or at least the goal pages and an IEP snapshot (see Figure 1.1, Chapter 1, Getting Organized). These people are an integral part of the IEP team and must have access to the academic plan for each student. Service providers such as speech pathologists and physical or occupational therapists will have copies of the goals and objectives specific to their area of service, but make a copy of all the goals and objectives available to them if needed.

▶ 4. The IEP will include a statement of any special education and related services and supplementary aids and services that are to be provided for the child to help him or her meet the IEP goals. In addition, each child with special needs is entitled to participate in the general curriculum and other school activities with children who are nondisabled, if possible. As the special education teacher, you are the advocate for the students you teach, and it is part of your responsibility to be sure they receive the services to which they are entitled. If you feel your school is not providing these for your students, consult with your special education supervisor who should be able to help you.

▶ 5. Most children with special needs will participate in state- and districtwide assessments. An IEP page will address this and list any accommodations needed for the child when he or she takes the assessments. For example, the student may need to have extended time or short breaks during testing. A small number of students will not take these tests because of their particular needs. In this case, the IEP team will determine that such students will take an alternate assessment. It is your responsibility as the special education teacher to look at the IEP and to be aware of the assessment status for each of your students. Check it for the accommodations necessary for those students taking the tests and for the alternate assessments for students who will not be taking them. Do this at the beginning of the school year—don't wait until a week before testing begins to gather this information. Also, be sure to let the general education teachers know the assessment status of each student with disabilities in their classroom.

Planning for Academic and Behavioral Success

As the special education teacher, you need to be sure to provide certain information to the general education teacher so that students with disabilities will gain maximum benefit from the general education classroom setting. If you feel overwhelmed by this responsibility, read on to see how you can effectively accomplish this task.

▶ 1. You should consider three areas—academics, behavior management, and grading—when you talk with the general education teacher about how students with special education needs can make the most of their experience in the general education classroom. Do this as soon as possible, and be sure the general education teacher has the students' IEP goals and objectives as a reference. Remember that collaboration should continue throughout the school year, and also be aware that it may be up to you to keep the communication ongoing.

▶ 2. If your students are in a general education setting for all or most of their academic instruction, it would be ideal to have access to lesson plans so you know what is ahead for them. For various reasons, however, this may not always be possible. If lesson plans are unavailable to you, another way to obtain information is to provide the general education teacher with a form on which he or she can indicate upcoming academic lessons (see Figure 1.2, Chapter 1, Forms and Schedules). You can provide the most assistance to your students by being up to date on what they are learning, and it is important for you to make every effort to get this data.

▶ 3. If you are able to access lesson information ahead of time, you will have more opportunity to adapt tasks or provide alternate assignments. This can be crucial for the success of your students with disabilities and should be a real incentive for you to obtain this information in advance. Usually, special education teachers are the ones responsible for making lesson modifications or accommodations. General education teachers will be appreciative of your efforts in this area as they are usually very busy with their responsibilities to their students. Be open, however, to any suggestions or ideas they may have about how to help students with disabilities succeed. If you are concerned about how to make adaptations for your students, visit a teaching supply store—most have whole sections for special education where you are likely to find the help you need.

▶ 4. Often, it is the responsibility of the special education teacher to develop a behavior management system for students with disabilities in the general education classroom. However, since the general education teacher will probably be the one to implement the plan most of the time, be sure to include this person in its development. Follow the IEP goals and objectives and the behavior plan if the student has one. Then, create something that is realistic and has a good chance of being successful. Review the plan with the general education teacher every few weeks to decide whether it's still working or if it needs revamping. Your willingness to address behavior problems and to follow through on reviewing and revamping the plan if needed will make you a hero in the eyes of your general education colleague.

▶ 5. Grading for students with special education needs can be done in several ways, but often the general and special education teachers collaborate on this. Sometimes, an alternative grading system will be used that is based on the extent of the adaptations made to the general curriculum. There are several alternative ways to grade students. Below are some for your consideration. (The information below is from Vasa [1981] and another source that the authors were unable to identify.)

    a. Points can be given for assignments, with a total number of points designated for an A, B, C, and so on.

    b. Shared grading means that both teachers decide on the grade—the percentage depending on the adaptations that must be made to the general curriculum.

    c. A contract with the student allows the student to complete certain parts of an assignment for a specific grade. For example, to earn an A grade, the entire assignment (possibly with accommodations or modifications) must be completed. To earn a B grade, one part may be omitted, and to earn a C grade, the student can choose to do a more limited part of the assignment. The teacher(s) should decide on what the student must accomplish to earn a specific grade, and this may differ for each student.

    d. IEP grading is a way to measure the student's competency levels based on his or her IEP goals and objectives, which can then be interpreted based on the district standards. For example, if IEP objectives under a certain goal require 90% accuracy and that range translates into a grade of B on the district scale, then the student would receive that grade in the IEP goal area.

    e. Mastery-level criterion grading means that a student earns a grade when his or her skill level has reached a certain level. For example, if the criterion indicates that 32/40 is a passing math grade, and the student meets or betters that criterion, he or she will earn a passing grade for that skill.

f. Using a multiple grading system means that the student is evaluated in several different criteria such as ability, effort, and achievement—you may decide on other areas. For example, a student could receive 20 points for completing the assignment on time, 40 points for including all sections of the project, and 40 points for using five or more resources.

Coteaching and Coplanning

The reality of coplanning and coteaching is that it is often not a 50–50 proposition. As the special education teacher, you may need to be the one to put forth extra effort. But it will pay off for your students with disabilities, for you, and for students in the general education classroom if you do.

▶ 1. Depending on how your school implements services to students with special needs, you may or may not be involved in teaching whole-group lessons in the classroom. If you do share teaching responsibilities with the general education teacher, you may be doing double duty—you will need to prepare a lesson for the entire class and also be sure that your students with special education needs are keeping up. If you are working in the general education classroom and doing part of the teaching, you may want to do the following.

a. Work with your general education colleague to find a time to touch base about expectations for the lesson. Everyone's time is limited, so don't assume you will be able to have a lengthy discourse. Even a few minutes can help clarify expectations and provide time to evaluate the success of the lesson. Make an effort to meet once a week—you may have to work around your colleague's schedule. But even if it inconveniences you a bit, it will be worth your while to feel organized and clear about what will happen during the lesson.

b. Decide how you will meet your obligations to your students with special education needs. Will you provide written material in advance that they can read to prepare ahead for the lesson? Will the general education teacher supervise these students while you are teaching? Will you use the buddy system and ask students in the general education classroom to assist those with disabilities? Will you make adaptations to seatwork or other activities that are part of the lesson? Plan this in advance to be sure you are meeting the IEP goals and objectives of your students with special education needs.

c. Often, if one person is the lead teacher, the other will handle discipline problems should they occur. Be sure to decide how you will manage this with your coteacher so that if a student's behavior becomes an issue, the lesson can still proceed smoothly.

▶ 2. If you are coteaching a lesson, take time with your partner to consider how you will handle the following lesson components: monitoring the transition to the lesson, introducing the lesson, teaching the lesson, monitoring independent work time, bringing closure to the lesson, transitioning to the next activity, and grading the written assignments. In addition, it is vital to verbally reinforce each other during the lesson by clarifying the subject matter—that is, repeating important information and asking for questions. Doing these things strengthens what is being taught for the students. Sometime after the lesson, take time with your teaching partner to jointly assess its successes and failures.

▶   3.   Collaborate with your general education colleague on what kind of ongoing evaluation you will use for students with special education needs. It is best not to wait until report card time to decide how you will grade your students. Keep written records of grades as well as some work samples as evidence. Ongoing evaluation with input from each teacher involved will make report card time much less stressful, as you will have a solid basis for the grades you assign.

▶   4.   If teachers do not have time to plan together, they may want to use the collaboration and coteaching lesson plan form (Figure 5.1). This worksheet can be used in two ways. First, if coteaching, the general education teacher fills in the lesson specifics, and then the special education teacher adds adaptations for certain students. Both teachers should initial who will be responsible for which part of the lesson. Second, the special education teacher can use the sheet to make adaptations for the students with disabilities so the general education teacher has them available to be implemented when needed during the lesson. Though this can be a very valuable resource to use, you may think it takes too much time to complete or might be unrealistic for other reasons. If this is true, consider the following ways to modify its use.

   a.   If you are unable to get the general education teacher to complete his or her portion of the form, at least gather as much verbal information as possible regarding lesson content. Then, make some notes on the special education teacher side for yourself as a reminder of things you may want to do for your students.

   b.   When you discuss the lesson with your general education partner, be sure to decide on how to divide up the teaching responsibilities. Being coordinated and organized in this aspect of the lesson is very important because behavior problems can erupt when teachers are confused and lessons are poorly planned. Use the worksheet to jot down parts of the lesson you will teach.

   c.   The worksheet can also be used to help the general education teacher when you are not in the classroom. Sharing some of your techniques for adapting work or dealing with behavior with your teaching partner can be done by leaving a copy of your worksheet for him or her. Giving verbal advice to peers can sometimes create a delicate situation. But if you leave a copy of your lesson worksheet on their desk, they can decide privately whether they want or need your suggestions.

   d.   If you are using a resource model—working with small groups within or outside the classroom—the coteaching lesson plan can be helpful. You can use the lesson specifics entered on the plan by the general education teacher to help you make adaptations for your students with special education needs.

▶   5.   If you stay in the classroom to teach small groups, be sure you consider the following advice, as it can help the general education teacher view you as a welcome addition rather than a disruption. Find a relatively quiet area in the room

Figure 5.1   Collaboration and Coteaching Lesson Plan

Collaboration and Coteaching Lesson Plan

Subject	Lesson	Modifications	Teacher
Objective(s)			
Materials			
Introduction, Content/ Activities			
Lesson Closure/ Transition			
Co-Assessment			

Source: Judy Walker-Wied, 2000

that provides adequate space for your group. Have all of your supplies and material on hand so you don't waste time getting organized while your students become disruptive waiting for you. Use a behavior program if needed to help keep your students focused and quiet as they work, and be sure you have a strategy for transitioning to and from the lesson that allows only minimal disruption to the class as a whole.

Adapting Lessons

Students with special education needs frequently require adaptations including accommodations or modifications to their lessons to help them succeed. Confused by these three terms and how to use them correctly? Read on.

▶   1. *Adaptation* is a term that covers changes of any kind to lessons that will help students with disabilities to learn. There are two kinds of adaptations—accommodations and modifications.

   a. *Accommodations* are adjustments that help students with lesser disabilities without changing content, expectations, or activities. An example of this would be more time to complete an assignment or taping a section of a text that is being used by the class for a lesson. Usually, accommodations are acceptable for use during standardized testing.

   b. *Modifications* are changes to the general education curriculum that impact the content, expectations, or activities. An example of this would be to have a student with disabilities read a book on the same topic as his or her counterpart in the general education classroom but at a different reading level. Usually, modifications are not acceptable for use during standardized testing.

▶   2. As a special education teacher, it is usually your responsibility to make accommodations or modifications for your students with disabilities. If you work in a general education classroom, there may be students other than those with disabilities who can benefit from this kind of help. Another way to be a hero in the eyes of your general education colleague is to provide this extra help for some of these students. But remember that your first obligation is to your students with disabilities. If you are at a loss as to how to adapt lessons, look in the Suggested Readings in the back of this book for resources that can help. Also, most teaching supply stores have a section for special education. Browse through—there are many useful resources.

▶   3. Be sensitive to how much and what kind of adaptations your students need. For example, don't assume that a student who has difficulty finishing a full page of addition doesn't understand how to add. He or she may simply need a more limited number of problems to complete. Sometimes a whole page can seem overwhelming, and this small accommodation can solve the problem. Be sensitive also to when a student may no longer need an adaptation. Your math student's confidence may build, and soon he or she may be able to complete an entire page. Think about the minimum number of adaptations a student may need so that you don't provide more help than necessary.

Accessing the General Education Curriculum

Helping your students access the general education curriculum is probably one of the most important parts of your job. Depending on the ability level of the student, there are several ways this can be done. Look below for service delivery suggestions.

▶ 1. Students' IEPs will indicate the subjects in which they will require instruction from a special education teacher. The IEP team will also have indicated if the subject is to be taught in the general education classroom or in a special education setting. In making these determinations, the team considers the strengths and areas of need of the student in relation to the least restrictive environment. Academic areas indicated in the IEP are those where adaptations need to be made by the special education teacher. In the best-case scenario, you will adapt the material at or near the student's grade level. However, the reality often is that students with disabilities may be functioning considerably below grade level.

▶ 2. Students with special education needs who are functioning near grade level can often access the general education curriculum in the classroom by participating in lessons with only limited accommodations. So remember to be sensitive to how much help they really need. Your objective should be to allow students to do as much as they can on their own. With students who are working at this level, you may or may not feel you need to be in the general education classroom. This decision is best made by you and the general education teacher. Of course, you will need to touch base regularly with both the general education teacher and your student to be sure learning is taking place.

▶ 3. The needs of students who are functioning well below grade level may best be served in a small group where the subject matter reflects one of their IEP goals. There may also be students from the general education classroom who can benefit from working in this kind of group. Your willingness to include them in your groups can be beneficial in several ways. Your students with disabilities will not be totally separated from those in the general education classroom, extra help will be provided for needy students, and your willingness to include these students will not go unnoticed by the general education teacher. Students with disabilities who need a small-group setting will probably require more extensive modifications to their lessons. If there is a teacher assistant assigned to your program, you may want to consider having that person work with a small group if you are involved in other teaching duties. But be sure you plan the lesson and that you are confident your assistant is capable of this assignment. (Please note that titles for persons assisting teachers in their classrooms may be different in your school district.)

▶ 4. A smaller percentage of students with special education needs will access the general curriculum entirely or almost entirely in the special education classroom. The IEP team will have determined that the student's needs can best be met there. However, very few students should remain in this classroom for their entire school day. As the special education teacher, you should make every effort to explore ways your students can be included in some general education classroom experiences. You may be able to start with inclusion in a special class such as art, music, or gym. If this inclusive experience is successful, you may want to consider trying the student in an academic subject. You may want to incorporate the use of an academic contract for students who are included to some degree in a general education classroom. This contract could target certain skills or concepts important for the student to learn in a specified amount of time (Figure 5.2).

▶ 5. Remember to be sure you make necessary changes to the student's IEP if the method of service delivery for a subject area has changed in any way. This will mean that the IEP team might need to reconvene to document the changes. The parent must be included as a member of the team. (Note that IDEA 2004 provides more flexibility for parents and schools by allowing them to agree to make minor changes in a child's IEP without reconvening the IEP team. However, be sure to check with your school district to determine if or how this will be implemented.)

 Many schools do not offer general education programming for three-year-olds. So, if you are an early childhood special education teacher, these students will probably be in your classroom for the entire day. You may find some success with inclusion of four-year-olds, as most schools have K4 programming.

Transition Times

Transition times are often unstructured, and the resulting chaos can affect the next lesson. In classrooms with small groups of students working in various areas, transitions can be hectic. If your classroom is out in the hallway, things can be even more difficult. Consider these suggestions to help keep everyone calm.

▶ 1. Movements by a student or a group of students from one activity to another can take place within a lesson, within the classroom, or going to or from a classroom in the school building. Smooth transitions can happen only if they are well thought out by the teacher beforehand. Transition-time behavior needs to be taught to all children, starting with the first day of school, and then modeled for them and practiced by them. Some students with special needs may require a cue or head start to complete transitions successfully.

▶ 2. Be sure to build transition time into your lessons, especially when working with students with disabilities. Some of them have difficulty staying focused in unstructured situations and are easily distracted, so you may need more time for doing this. Whatever your classroom situation, give advance notice to your students about an upcoming transition. You may want to say, "You have 1 more minute to complete your math problems before we take out our English books." If you are able to add, "There will be time later in the day for those who are not finished to complete their work," it can prevent students from ignoring your directions to hurry and finish.

▶ 3. Be specific about how you expect your group to transition. You may find it best to give only one- or two-step directions, and then wait for students to

Figure 5.2   Reaching My Goal

My Goal for _____

This week, I will

1. _____

2. _____

3. _____

If I reach my goal, I will be able to

_____

_____

_____

My teacher will help me by

_____

_____

Signed by

_____Student

_____Teacher

_____Date

Source: Jill Lindberg, 2004

comply before you continue. Sometimes even older students do better when directions are simplified and extra time is given to carry them out. If some students have difficulty understanding what to do, use a buddy system. Have someone nearby who is reliable help put papers away in the correct folder or accompany the student to the assigned spot in line.

▶   4.   Transitions to other classrooms, the bathroom, cafeteria, playground, or the bus require teaching, modeling—and practice. Sometimes students with special education needs have difficulty standing in line or walking while keeping their mouth and body quiet. Model for them, and teach specifically what you expect. Ask other students, including your students with disabilities, to demonstrate appropriate hallway behavior. Limit your expectations—quiet mouths, hands to yourself, walk directly behind the person in front of you. These simple, specific directions leave little room for misunderstanding and are easily observable by you.

▶   5.   Define what is expected. Call students by tables or rows, and verbally reinforce their appropriate movements. Team rewards for groups or rows will reinforce successful transitions. If some of your students with disabilities have difficulty with transitions, consider working with them as a group to develop a plan to help them. Include appropriate rewards for success. Students who transition from one classroom to another by themselves need to know and learn the expectation for movement in the hallway. Communication between teachers is important. Use of a classroom phone to notify the receiving teacher may work when the student is going from one room to another. Or give the student a note to take to the next class that states the time the student has left the room along with the date and teacher's signature.

With students in an early childhood classroom, visual cues are especially useful. Use a timer with a visual component, so students are aware of how much time is left before a transition. You can also use picture cues for each activity of the school day. Pictures of typical school-related activities can be found in *Boardmaker*, which is a computer software program that provides a wide variety of simple, clear pictures for classroom use. Copy and mount appropriate pictures, and put them in a place where you frequently gather your students. Introduce them at the beginning of the day. Then remove them as each activity is completed, so the children can anticipate what will happen as the day progresses.

Define spaces for these students by taping cutouts to the floor in the shape of feet so they will know where to line up. You can cover these cutouts with clear, plastic, adhesive-backed paper to preserve them. (You might want to check with your building maintenance person to see if placing adhesive paper on the floor is acceptable.)

Special Education Instructional Planning

As a special education teacher, your duties may be more varied than those of your general education counterpart. In the same hour, you may be teaching one student, a small group, and a whole class. Whether you are working in the general classroom or with a group of students with special education needs, effective instruction is paramount. It is important to have a framework to use each time you plan your lessons to help assure that you carefully consider how you will manage each part. The following conceptual framework for effective instruction applies to teaching one student, a small group, or an entire class (from Ysseldyke, Algozzine, & Thurlow, 2000, p. 198).

▶   1.   Plan the instruction. Decide what to teach by identifying your lesson objectives. If you are teaching a whole-group lesson in the general education classroom, decide how you can relate these objectives to the IEP goals for your students with disabilities. If you are teaching one student or a small group, you can more specifically target your instructional planning to the students' IEP goals. But whatever your situation, be sure to consider the learning requirements of your students with special education needs.

▶ 2. Manage the instruction by deciding what methods you will use to teach the lesson. When planning this, consider the different learning styles students have. Provide visual, auditory, and kinesthetic components to your lessons when possible. Varying the presentation of the material and any connected activities will also address the different ways students learn. Teacher-directed lessons or students working independently, in pairs, or in small groups are ways to help foster success for all students. Concluding with whole-group feedback is a way for you to gauge the success of your lesson.

▶ 3. Deliver the instruction with an eye to student comprehension—whether a whole class or small group, read their faces. Are they focused? What do their expressions tell you? Ask for students to restate what they heard, give examples, demonstrate on the board, or work problems to check understanding. Don't move on if you think there are a number of students who are confused. If you are in a whole-class setting, realize you may need to review materials later with your students with disabilities, as well as with others who may need further clarification.

▶ 4. Evaluate the instruction throughout the lesson, especially when students are working on a new concept. Assess individually as you circulate around the classroom or as you monitor your group. Pair a strong student with one who needs extra help or guidance, but check on them as they work to be sure they are on task. Watching students work individually can be a valuable way of assessing the effectiveness of your lesson.

Your Involvement in the General Education Classroom

Do you feel like persona non grata when you enter the general education classroom? It's up to you to change that and become an important contributor to the education of all students. Here's how you can accomplish this important goal.

▶ 1. The first step is to note your students' grade levels and in how many different classrooms they are placed. Ideally, working between two and four classrooms is best. If students have not already been placed, you may want to take time to discuss this with your principal. If it's too late for this school year, make a note to do so for next year. Be an advocate for appropriate services for your students. If they are spread out over too many classrooms, you may want to consider combining those that can work together into one classroom or other area during specific subjects or time frames.

▶ 2. It is important to meet with all of the general education teachers to plan your involvement in their classroom. In some schools, there are regularly scheduled grade-level meetings, and you should join those in which your students are placed. But set up your own meeting if there are no grade-level meetings at your school. Ask for weekly schedules, and together with the general education teacher, decide when it would be appropriate for you to provide support within the general education setting. Your involvement could range from teaching whole-class lessons to providing assistance for students with special education needs and others that could gain from your services. You may be the one to adapt lessons for all students who could benefit, or you may work with small groups within the classroom. These are decisions best made by you and the general education teacher in a way that will be mutually comfortable for both of you and beneficial to all the students.

▶ 3. IEPs are the guidelines for the education of students with disabilities. It is extremely important that the general education teachers are able to read and understand them because they are also responsible for their implementation. Be sure each teacher has a copy of the IEPs for all students with special education needs. Plan a time, if possible, to review these with the teacher, and address questions and concerns. Provide an IEP snapshot or another way for the teacher to quickly reference this pertinent information (see Figure 1.1, Chapter 1, Student Information).

▶ 4. If a teacher assistant is assigned to work in classrooms with your special education students, make certain that person's time is used wisely. (Please note that titles for persons assisting teachers in their classrooms may be different in your school district.) Meet with that person and the general education teacher to discuss the assistant's role within the classroom and how students can benefit from this assistance. Create a schedule for this person that involves teacher-directed, student-connected activities. Maximum involvement with students should be the goal for your assistant. The more help a student with special needs receives, the more progress he or she will make. But make sure your assistant understands he or she is to work *with* the students, not do the work *for* the students.

▶ 5. Finally, here are some tips that will facilitate your success and the success of your students with disabilities in the general education classroom: Remain flexible regarding your involvement in that setting. Be willing to reassess and make changes. When thinking about rewards and negative consequences, remember that everything works—for a while. Students are diverse regardless of disabilities, so keep that in mind and remain open to change. Also, keep channels of communication fluid between yourself and the colleagues with whom you work. Be willing to give and take. This is the vehicle for success within the inclusive classroom, and without it you may find yourself alone in the struggle to help your students. You don't need to be best friends with everyone, but it is important to make an effort to remain professional and work collaboratively.

Record Keeping and Information Management

S ince accountability has become the byword in education today, record keeping has taken on new importance—especially for special education teachers. But being that it is only one of a myriad of tasks that must be addressed, finding a way to make it manageable is a must. Since hiring a secretary of your own is not an option, try some of the suggestions in this chapter to meet this ongoing challenge.

Chapter Outline

- Creating a System
- Finding Time to Complete Paperwork
- IEPs and Progress Reports
- Report Cards and Grading

Creating a System

There is so much information teachers need at their fingertips that creating a system to keep things organized and up to date is critical. What works for one person may not work for another, so finding a method that is manageable for you is very important. But whatever system you use, be sure to include the following important information.

▶   1. Since there is often a great deal of information needed for each student, you may want to consider using pocket folders, file folders, or one large binder with pocket-type inserts, one for each student. Folders or binders with pockets will allow you to add information—even if you just jot something on a slip of paper and stick it in the pocket to be dealt with later. It works best to have all necessary information for one student in one place and easily accessible to you. Then, when talking about a student with other teachers, support staff, parents, or even your principal, you have everything you need at hand. But remember, this information is private. It should not be lying on your desk for all to see. Keep it handy in a file drawer that you can easily access during the day, and then put it in a place that can be locked up for the night.

▶   2. The following information about each student should always be easily accessible for you: full name of the student, student's birth date, school identification number, full names of the parents (their last names may be different from each other's or different from the student's), current address and phone number (these may change during the school year, so be sure to keep up to date), parents' work phone numbers and information about contacting them there; information about who can have physical contact with the child (sometimes a parent or family member cannot), and medical information—especially regarding allergies or medication the child must take at school. All of this may be available on computer if your district has a computerized IEP and data system. Be aware that there may be other information your school system or district deems important. If your school asks students or their family members to complete emergency cards at the beginning of the year, make copies of them for your own records before they are sent to the office. They contain a good deal of valuable, up-to-date information—and it's all in one place.

▶   3. In addition to the aforementioned data, you will also want to have copies of all documentation related to the student's IEP. In most school systems, the IEP itself is often placed in the student's cumulative folder that goes with the student from grade to grade. However, you should have your own copy for your files. Other things you will want, if they apply to any of your students, include copies of medical information, FBAs, and BIPs. These items may also be on a districtwide computer system. Someone in your school office will know, as will special education personnel in the building. If your district has this software, learn how to use it—training is probably offered.

▶   4. Another crucial system you will want to create is one for scheduling IEP meetings. One way to do this is by using a daily desk calendar. This kind of calendar, of course, is very helpful for keeping track of all kinds of information. But using it as a way to keep up to date on IEP meetings can be very helpful. Make a note (perhaps in red or another bright color) of all IEP annual review or triennial evaluation dates. Also indicate when parent invitations for which you are responsible need to be sent out—usually well in advance of the IEP meeting. You may also want to include a reminder to send invitations to other staff members involved in the meeting. You might even want to jot on your calendar something like, "Terrell's annual IEP on 3/10/06" a week or so beforehand, just to be sure you haven't forgotten. You can use the same system with a large, on-the-desk calendar—just don't cover it with so many papers that you can't see what you have written. Because IEPs are legal documents, it is imperative that you develop some system to help you keep track of what you must do and when you must do it.

Finding Time to Complete Paperwork

Stop daydreaming about getting a secretary, and be realistic about how you can manage that mound of paperwork that only seems to grow. Think about your daily schedule—sometimes a few moments here and there can add up to enough time to make a real dent in that pile. Read on for some helpful ideas.

▶ 1. Begin by thinking about what you need to get done on a weekly basis. This may be easier and more practical than to think day by day. Then review your schedule, and try to find free time each day when you can begin to chip away at your duties. Keep a list of weekly paperwork and other responsibilities (phone calls, contacts with other professionals, and so on), and check them off when completed—a kind of positive reinforcement for yourself.

▶ 2. If you have a computer in your room where you can work on IEPs and other documentation, keep a file folder nearby containing guidelines and completed samples of various paperwork so you have some examples when you work. This can be a real time-saver and will allow you to make the best use of every precious moment.

▶ 3. If you don't mind coming in a little early or staying after school, you may find that this can be a quiet time with few interruptions when you can accomplish a great deal. If you are willing to give up 15 or 20 minutes of your lunch hour, this can also be a relatively peaceful time when you can concentrate on paperwork. As a special education teacher, you should be allowed some prep time on a weekly basis to use for paperwork completion. You may want to discuss this with your principal or special education supervisor.

▶ 4. Some school districts have IEP software that can be installed on home computers. You may feel less pressure if you can do this important work at home. Check with your special education administrator to see if there is something like this available for you to use. Schools might also have laptop computers with downloaded IEP software that can be taken home by staff to use to write IEPs. Talk to your technology coordinator to see if this is accessible to you.

▶ 5. Remember also that phone calling can be done at home. You may feel less stressed if you make a few calls in the evening. So be sure you know which parents can be reached at that time, and make it a point to phone them then. As a result, there will be a few less contacts you need to make at school.

IEPs and Progress Reports

Understanding the often-changing IEP procedures can be confusing and sometimes stressful—especially for new teachers. Don't make guesses when

completing these important legal documents. There should be resource people in your school who can help and provide you with accurate information. Look below for additional suggestions.

▶ 1. In many cases, individual school districts have their own format and procedures for IEPs. Most districts offer inservice training for teachers to help them keep up with the latest changes—be sure to take advantage of these. Since IEPs are legal documents—this means that attorneys can use them in court cases—it is imperative that you keep abreast of any format or procedural changes. Watch for opportunities in your district to find out about the newly reauthorized IDEA 2004 legislation. You will need to be aware of changes that will directly affect you. You can access some of this information on the following Web site: http://www.wrightslaw.com.

▶ 2. If you are a new teacher or even an experienced teacher who has questions about how to complete the IEP, do not hesitate to seek the advice of other professionals who can provide correct information. This can include veteran special education teachers or the special education administrator in your building. Don't be too proud to seek out the accurate information you need to write a legally correct IEP. Then, as noted in the strategy in this chapter titled Finding Time to Complete Paperwork, keep written guidelines and a copy of a correctly written IEP at hand as a model.

▶ 3. Remember that if your students with special needs spend time in a general education classroom, the general education teachers must be asked to contribute to the development of the IEP. Solicit ideas and suggestions from them, as they are an integral part of the IEP team. Another important thing to remember about IEPs and the IEP planning meeting is that this document should be brought to the meeting with the idea that it is a work in progress at this point. Team members, especially any family present, should be encouraged to contribute by adding or changing anything they deem necessary. When the meeting is finished, and based on the procedures in your district, family members should receive a copy of the completed IEP before they leave the meeting. Or a corrected clean copy should be mailed to them as soon as possible.

▶ 4. Many school districts require IEP progress notes that must be sent to parents with no less frequency than traditional report cards—be sure you know your district's policy on this. If this is a requirement for you, see if there is a form for this information. It might include a place to assign a grade for progress made on IEP goals as well as room for the teacher's remarks. This brief teacher's narrative portion is an important part of the progress report. Be sure to comment on both successes and areas that need improvement for the student. Consider including a brief statement about how parents can support your efforts in an area of need for their child at home. And be sure to ask for input from the general education teacher.

▶ 5. Above all, remember that both the IEP and the progress notes should be true indications of what the student needs to accomplish academically. They should include information on his or her strengths and areas needing improvement that are reflected in the goals and objectives. No two students are the same; no two IEPs or progress notes should look the same.

Report Cards and Grading

For students with special education needs, report cards should help complete the picture of the student's academic progress. School districts vary with their expectations for report cards and for grading students with special needs. But there are some things that every special education teacher should consider when report card time rolls around.

▶ 1. Collecting a body of work that provides evidence for students' progress is imperative when planning for report card grading. (Some schools have a portfolio assessment system already in place.) Start early in the year, and keep a file for each of your students. It isn't necessary to save every piece of paper they generate. Choose work that shows significant evidence of progress and skill development—or lack thereof—especially in the areas of their IEP goals. Keep brief notes about class participation, social interaction, and behavior. Then, at report card time, you won't have to rely on your memory.

▶ 2. If your students are in an inclusive setting, you most likely work with a general education teacher and will need to collaborate with that person on the report cards for them. Neither of you should shoulder the sole responsibility for deciding on grades for the students with special education needs. Both of you can bring a unique perspective on their social, behavioral, and academic success. Work as a team to decide how these students can be portrayed accurately in their report cards. And remember that if you are in a general education classroom only part of the time, the general education teacher may actually spend more time with your student(s) than you do.

▶ 3. As noted, every school district has a different way of grading students with special education needs. Be sure you are aware of your district's criteria. Often, grades reflect progress on students' IEP goals. In areas that are not part of the IEP such as social studies; science; and special classes including art, music, and physical education—there may be others in your school district—you may want to collaborate with your general education partner to develop a grading rubric.

▶ 4. One way to think about grading for students with special education needs who are considerably below grade level in all subject areas is to use their beginning-of-the-year skills as a baseline. Then grade your students throughout the school year on the progress you see. In other words, compare your students to themselves only, and not to what others in the class are doing. It is difficult to equate the progress of students who are functioning significantly below grade level with students who are on or near grade level. The work samples you have collected, and your notes on social and behavioral progress, should provide you with the evidence you need to compare the student's progress to the baseline you have established for him or her.

▶ 5. There are other formats you can use to grade your students and additional resources to help you decide what to do. Refer to Chapter 5, Planning for Academic and Behavioral Success, for alternative evaluation ideas. Again, your district may have a set grading formula for students with special education needs, so be sure you are aware of it if there is one. You can also ask other special education teachers or someone from your special education administrative team for ideas.

Report cards for students with special education needs in an early childhood classroom will usually contain different information than those for students in higher grades. Check to see if your school uses a different report card format for younger students. Even if your school uses the same report card for all grade levels, there is usually space for a short narrative where you can include information that is more specific to young children.

Some school districts also have a format for indicating progress on IEP goals that is separate from the traditional report card. This can also provide an opportunity for you to address development of the younger child in addition to showing progress on IEP goals.

As you complete these report forms, remember to write your information in parent-friendly language. Professional and legal terminology can be confusing to lay persons.

Legal Issues

7

The legal responsibilities for a special education teacher can be daunting, and in many districts the paperwork addressing these legal issues is complex and changes from year to year. Since each school district and each state has its own method of interpreting how some of these issues should be addressed, this chapter will not discuss specifics. But read on for helpful ideas that can apply generally.

Chapter Outline

- IDEA Reauthorization
- Functional Behavior Assessment (FBA)
- Behavior Intervention Plan (BIP)
- Manifestation Determination
- Student and Parent Rights
- Suspensions

IDEA Reauthorization

Special education teachers must wear many hats today. Understanding and keeping current with the latest legal issues that affect teaching students with special education needs is only one of them—but a very important one. Here's a minilesson.

(The information about IDEA 2004 came from the State of Wisconsin Department of Public Instruction. The Web address is http://www.dpi.state.wi.us. Please be sure you are aware of changes in the new IDEA 2004 legislation that your district will implement that can affect you as a teacher. You can access more information on IDEA 2004 by going to the following Web site: http://www.wrightslaw.com.)

▶   1.   Historically, Public Law 94-142 (Education of All Handicapped Children Act) assures that all children with handicapping conditions are entitled to a free and appropriate public education in the least restrictive environment to meet their unique needs. As of July 1, 2005, the newly reauthorized IDEA 2004 is in effect. (IDEA 2004 is the Individuals with Disabilities Education Improvement Act.) The reauthorization addresses areas including, but not limited to, continued and increased parental involvement in decisions on their child's education; establishing, expanding, or increasing the use of systemic positive behavioral school interventions by teachers and administrators; reducing paperwork; and continued education for teacher assistants who work with children with special needs.

▶   2.   Children ages 3 to 21 are protected by IDEA. The child must be at least 3 years old but not yet 21 and not yet graduated from high school. To qualify under IDEA, a child must meet three criteria, which would be identified at the time of the child's Individualized Education Program (hereinafter referred to as IEP) meeting and in the written copies of the document.
    a.   The child must be handicapped as identified in one or more of the categories of impairment defined in IDEA.
    b.   This impairment must adversely affect the child's educational performance.
    c.   The qualified impairment must require special education and related services.

▶   3.   Federal law dictates that the IEP process, from the written referral to the IEP meeting to determine special education needs, may not take more than 60 calendar days, and a placement determination must be made within 90 days of the receipt of consent from parent or guardian. This time line refers to both the initial IEP process as well as reevaluations. Be aware that your state law may be different. The school can request and be granted an extension if there is reasonable need. The parent or guardian must give written permission for any evaluations done on the child.

▶   4.   IDEA requires the development of an IEP document with specific content to address the child's education needs. The law also requires that the IEP team consist of the parents of the student, at least one general education teacher familiar with the student, at least one special education teacher, and a representative of the Local Education Agency (LEA), who is usually a school administrator. There is an initial meeting to determine if the child requires special education services. Then a meeting is held annually, and a reevaluation of special education needs is done every three years. The parents or guardian have a legal right to be invited to all meetings. (Please note that IDEA 2004 provides greater flexibility for parents and schools by allowing them to make minor changes to a child's IEP during the school year without reconvening the IEP team and by encouraging the consolidation of IEP and reevaluation meetings. Be sure you know your district's policy on implementing these changes.)

▶   5.   The following information has been newly added in the IDEA 2004 legislation and should be of interest to you as a teacher. Some or all of these may be implemented by your school district. Be sure to check with your school administrator or special education administrator for this information.

    a. A multiyear IEP may be an option, with consent from the parents or guardian. This IEP cannot exceed three years.

    b. There are two circumstances where IEP team participants may not need to attend an IEP team meeting if the parents or guardian agree in writing. First, a staff member can be excluded from attending if that person's area of the curriculum or related service is not being addressed at the meeting. Second, a staff member may be excluded if that person has submitted his or her information about the student in writing prior to the meeting.

    c. The number of reevaluations for a student is limited to one per year unless the parent or guardian and the LEA agree that another one is needed.

    d. IDEA 2004 requires schools to provide short-term objectives for students with significant disabilities and to report quarterly to parents of all students on their child's progress toward meeting his or her annual IEP goals. Be sure you know your district's policy on writing short-term objectives, as many districts will continue writing them for all students with disabilities.

Because your involvement in the IEP process means you are part of a legal process, it is imperative that you know your district's policy on implementing IDEA 2004 and that you understand your responsibilities and obligations. If you have any questions or concerns or are unsure of anything at all, be sure to talk to your principal or the special education administrator in your building.

Functional Behavior Assessment (FBA)

Sometimes a student's behavior becomes so serious that informal behavior programs don't work, and something more formal and intensive is needed. Don't be afraid to tackle a Functional Behavior Assessment. If done correctly and thoughtfully, it should provide what is needed to write a Behavior Intervention Plan that will be successful.

(The information about Functional Behavior Assessments and Behavior Intervention Plans came from the Milwaukee Public Schools Web site, http://www.milwaukeepublic schools.org and from Dr. James Larson, University of Wisconsin-Whitewater. Please be sure you are aware of changes in the new IDEA 2004 that may affect you as a teacher by accessing your state and district Web sites.)

▶   1. IDEA legislation requires that a Functional Behavior Assessment (hereinafter referred to as FBA) be completed if a student has been denied access to the implementation of his or her IEP for more than 10 days in a school year. The 10 days could result from suspension from either school or the bus. If the student is suspended from the bus that provides access to school, then he or she will be absent from school and will have been denied access to IEP implementation. Also be aware that if a student with special education needs is retained in the school office for disciplinary reasons, he or she must have work to do that is related to the IEP and must be around students from the general education classroom. The same holds true if the student is in a suspension room or a similar setting. If the student does not have work to do related to his or her IEP and is not around students from the general education classroom, the removal from class will count as part of the 10 days allowed. Be sure you know the policy in your district relating to the number of suspension days used before the FBA process must begin. Most districts do not wait until the 10th day to begin this process. Also note that to begin an FBA, an IEP meeting of all team members is called, and all required IEP paperwork is included.

▶ 2. The FBA is an analysis of what is happening to precipitate a certain behavior that a student displays. Usually, the behavior is seriously interfering with the student's learning, and the precipitating stimulus can be something in the school environment or something internal in the student. If it is possible to discover the stimulus causing the behavior, then it may be possible to change the behavior.

▶ 3. You as the special education teacher are responsible for initiating the FBA. Your administrator may or may not notify you about the number of days a student has been suspended from school, so it is best that you keep track of the suspensions of any students whom you feel may be close to reaching the 10-day limit. The IEP team must be reconvened to begin an FBA. Parents or a guardian must be invited, as well as other school professionals who would attend an annual review of the IEP.

▶ 4. During the first meeting, the inappropriate behavior must be defined in a very concrete way, including when and how often it happens. Be very specific when defining the target behavior. If there is more than one, pick the most obvious or the one that is causing the student the most difficulty in the school setting. Consider questions such as the following:
   a. Where is the student when the behavior occurs?
   b. What is the student doing when the behavior occurs?
   c. What students and adults are around when the behavior occurs, and what are they doing?
   d. What is the consequence for the behavior being displayed? (Most likely, the consequence is reinforcing the behavior.)
   e. Does the behavior entertain other students, or is the student asked to leave the classroom as a result of the behavior?

▶ 5. Then the team must decide how the data will be collected, by whom, and for how long. It is best to have at least three sources of data that will allow for cross-checking for validity. Below are listed three types of data collection methods. Your school district may choose to use others.
   a. A tally chart noting the activity and time during which the negative behavior most frequently occurs
   b. A problem behavior questionnaire completed by adults who work with the student
   c. A forced-choice reinforcement menu completed by the student to see what reinforces him or her

After the data has been collected and analyzed, a second meeting is held. This is also conducted just like an IEP annual review meeting, with all team members present and all necessary paperwork included. The information is shared to see if the data confirms the hypothesis. If everyone agrees that it does, the next step is to develop a Behavior Intervention Plan. If the evidence does *not* totally support the hypothesis, it may give enough information to provide an understanding of the exhibited behavior. If so, then this may be enough to develop a Behavior Intervention Plan. The Behavior Intervention Plan is usually formally written at this meeting, but team members can come with a draft.

Behavior Intervention Plan (BIP)

If an FBA is carefully and thoughtfully done, it should enable you to develop a Behavior Intervention Plan (hereinafter referred to as BIP) that can provide you with a successful way to eliminate—or at least greatly minimize—inappropriate behavior. Look below for some solid advice on how to make this happen.

▶ 1. The BIP is a plan of action that should enable you to replace the target inappropriate behavior with an acceptable behavior. It is important to use the data collected from the FBA to help determine how to develop the BIP. The function of the behavior must be understood before an appropriate intervention can be put in place, or the intervention will most likely fail. For example, if the student behaves in an acceptable manner until math time, is the behavior a result of the student not wanting to do math (a performance deficit) or not understanding how to do it (a skill deficit)?

▶ 2. The chosen intervention, based on the data from the FBA, will address either the performance deficit or the skill deficit displayed by the student. Remember that the BIP creates an intervention that does not depend on changes the student will make, but rather on changes to be made by the adults in the environment or changes in the instruction or curriculum that will effectively change the behavior of the student. The intervention should be proactive and positive in nature. It should be simple, not complex to implement, and one that can be supported by the adults involved in bringing about the desired change.

▶ 3. Remember to consider the student's strengths and how these can be supported in the plan. Make sure everyone included in the plan understands both his or her part in implementing it and the desired outcome. Each person should also know when the plan will begin to be used and how it will be monitored.

▶ 4. Be sure to identify periodic times to review the plan, and include this information within the plan. The BIP must be a working document. Input must come from all to determine if it is working well or if changes or modifications are needed. The success of the intervention depends on monitoring. Remember also that very few interventions last forever, so anticipate that a new one may need to be considered at some point.

Manifestation Determination

When a student with a disability commits a serious infraction of a school rule, he or she is subject to a different procedure from a student in the general education classroom. Be sure you are familiar with this process and who needs to be

involved. **Below is some basic information that may be helpful. (The information about manifestation determinations came from the State of Wisconsin Department of Public Instruction. The Web address is http://www.dpi.state.wi.us. Please be sure you are aware of any changes in the new IDEA 2004 legislation that your district will implement that can affect you as a teacher.)**

▶ 1. When a student with special education needs violates a school policy, it is the responsibility of the IEP team to determine if the violation was caused by or had a direct relationship to the student's disability, or if it was the direct result of the student's IEP not being implemented.

▶ 2. If the team, including the parents or guardian, determines that either of the two aforementioned situations applies, then the violation is considered to be a manifestation of the child's disability. In this case, the IEP team must proceed with a manifestation determination. The forms to be used for a manifestation determination will vary from district to district, so check with your special education administrator to see what is needed in your school.

▶ 3. When dealing with students who have behavior problems, the best plan is to be proactive—have an FBA and BIP in place. Then, when the IEP team convenes for a manifestation determination, the team can review the BIP and modify or change it as necessary. If an FBA and BIP are not in place for the child, the team must develop and implement them.

▶ 4. A manifestation determination is also held when a violation has put the student at the 10-day limit for denial of access to the IEP and the team needs to decide if a change in placement is necessary. The team may decide to return the student to the current placement or agree on a change in placement.

Student and Parent Rights

All students—including those in general education and those with special education needs—and their parents or guardians have rights within a school system. It is very important that all teachers are aware of what these rights are and that they understand them. Be sure to get this information from your school administration. Though these rights will differ from district to district across the country, the information below provides some examples of what may be included.

(The information about parents' rights came from the Milwaukee Public Schools Web site, http://www.milwaukeepublicschools.org and from the Cooperative Educational Service Agency 7 Web site, http://www.cesa7.k12.wi.us/sped. Access Web sites for your own state and school district for information specific to you. Please be sure you are aware of changes in the new IDEA 2004 that may affect you as a teacher.)

▶ 1. It is important for all teachers to know which family members have the legal right to access school information—or the legal right may belong to a guardian. Court-appointed guardians provide documents to the school indicating their rights in relation to the child. Legal guardians can attend IEP meetings and make school-related decisions for the student.

► 2. Most school districts provide parents or guardians with student handbooks and may also have a policy and procedure manual. Individual schools within the district may also have their own handbooks. Be sure to know what your school district provides, and obtain a copy of all relevant materials. Read them over, and familiarize yourself with anything that could pertain to your students. Note that many of the rules and regulations that affect students in the general education classroom also affect those with special education needs.

► 3. Parents should be the best advocates for their children. Below are some parent rights that are common to most school districts.
   a. The right to review their child's school records as well as to receive copies of information in the school records
   b. The right to expect that records and information about their child will be kept confidential
   c. The right to receive academic and attendance reports for their child
   d. The right to request conferences with teachers or administrators to review progress reports and attendance, disciplinary actions, tests, and so forth
   e. The right to visit the school and their child's classroom
   f. The right to have an interpreter if they are hearing impaired or if they do not speak English fluently

► 4. All parents or guardians—including parents or guardians of students with special education needs—have the right to due process if they have a complaint or concern. Ideally, parents or guardians should begin by working with the teacher and school principal. Usually, concerns can be resolved this way. If the parents or guardian is not satisfied with the outcome at the school level, they can be referred to a parent advocate. Many school districts have a parent information center that can provide this service.

► 5. In addition to those afforded all students, students with special education needs have additional rights. Most districts have this information available for parents or guardians of these students. Many systems require that parents' rights information is sent out with each IEP invitation and offered again at the IEP meeting. Some of the rights of parents or guardians of children with special needs include the following:
   a. To request and receive copies of individual IEP reports to review before the IEP meeting
   b. To be advised of procedural options by the IEP team if a concern is not addressed at the meeting
   c. To bring an advocate to an IEP meeting who can help parents or guardians understand their rights, explain procedures, and raise questions and concerns

Suspensions

A suspension should be a last resort—never the most frequently used negative consequence. And special education teachers must be mindful of the 10-day suspension limit for their students. Also, the effectiveness of a suspension can depend on several variables. Read on for some useful information.

(The information on suspensions came from the Milwaukee Public Schools Web site, http://www.milwaukeepublicschool.org. Access Web sites for your own state and school district for information specific to you. Please be sure you are aware of changes in the new IDEA 2004 that may affect you as a teacher.)

▶ 1. Suspensions can be a double-edged sword. For some students, they are effective ways to encourage appropriate behavior—for others, an opportunity to get away from school and spend an unproductive day at home. As a special education teacher, it is your job to know which one applies to which of your students. Suspensions should always be a last resort. Staying in the learning environment at school is almost always preferable to a day at home.

▶ 2. Students with special education needs may be suspended from school without service from their IEP for up to 10 days in one school year. All students—including students in the general education classroom—have the same due process procedures for suspension up to the 10th day. Students with special education needs have additional rights starting with the 11th day. At that point (or before, depending on your school district's policy), the IEP team must convene to either develop or review the FBA and BIP.

▶ 3. It is very important to note that an in-house suspension for a student with special education needs must provide for the implementation of his or her IEP and must allow for placement with peers from the general education classroom. Be sure you know your school's policy on in-house suspensions, and consider how effective the suspension will be in your school. The following are some guidelines that can help make in-house suspensions effective:
   a. The same set of policies should be enforced no matter who manages the suspension room.
   b. The adults in charge must convey the message that the suspension is not a social time. It must be a quiet, academically productive time.
   c. There should be guidelines in place for sending students to the suspension room. It should only be for students who have committed major infractions and for whom other negative classroom consequences have not worked.
   d. In-house suspensions should be short term, or they could begin to be a way to escape from the classroom for some students.

8

Working With Families

Working with family members is becoming an increasingly important part of any teacher's responsibilities. Striving to form a successful teacher–parent partnership can help provide an expanded understanding of the student that is helpful for any educator and can sometimes provide critical insight for a special education teacher. Consider the suggestions below as you decide on your approach to dealing with families.

Chapter Outline

- Before You Contact Families
- Establishing a Positive Relationship
- Ongoing Communication
- IEP Meetings
- Parent Conferences
- Documentation
- Assistance From School Support Staff

Before You Contact Families

Sometimes it can be a real challenge for special education teachers to establish and maintain a positive working relationship with family members. Families of

students with disabilities may be wary of contact with anyone from their child's school as it could have been unpleasant and contentious in the past. Your mission—should you decide to accept it—is to change that perception for the sake of your students. Read on for some helpful precontact tips.

▶ 1. At the beginning of the school year, take the time to look carefully through your students' cumulative folders and IEPs. Be sure you know the names and relationships of the child's family members. Sometimes the child and other family members will have different last names, or children may be living with relatives other than their parents. If parents are divorced, children may be spending time at different homes during the week. Check to see who has the legal right to make decisions for the child and who can have physical contact with him or her. Also, be sure you know whose name(s) is on the emergency contact card for your students.

▶ 2. Put all this information in a notebook of some kind that you can have at your fingertips if needed. But remember that this is confidential and should be kept in a private place. When you call family members, especially at first, you will want to avoid potential embarrassment by having all this necessary information at hand.

▶ 3. Keeping current with phone numbers is very important, but is often an ongoing challenge. To ensure that you have the correct information, you may want to call to obtain important numbers in addition to sending a form home to have family members complete. Sometimes there is no phone in the household, and you may want to ask if there is a neighbor or other family member living nearby. But be sure this person is willing to take phone calls, relay information, or get immediate family members to the phone. If you have a work number for a family member, check to be sure that it is permissible for you to call at work, and update this number periodically.

▶ 4. Remember also that home phones can be disconnected, and phone numbers may change during the school year. So you might want to check occasionally to see if any of these things have occurred. Also, ask if there is a certain time that is best to call at home, as some people work nights and sleep during the day. Rousing someone from sleep is not a good way to forge a positive relationship.

Establishing a Positive Relationship

Working with families who have children with special education needs can present a challenge beyond your work with the child him- or herself. Sensitivity and empathy are the bywords here. Remember, most families are doing their best for their child with the resources they have.

▶ 1. Families of children with special education needs frequently hear negative things from teachers. Make your first contact a positive one. Call to introduce yourself. Before you do, however, take time to think of something nice to say about the child. Be ready with some school goal for the child that he or she can probably achieve. Be sure to tell the family member you will be calling home with good news from time to time. This will prove to be a good investment when you need the family's support should problems arise.

▶ 2. Find out if the family would like some ongoing communication from you, whether it is in the form of a phone call, a note home, or just a smiley-face sticker on the child's shirt for a good day. Also, some families may have e-mail addresses and be willing to share them with you. If this is the case, be aware that sending e-mail is not necessarily a private transaction. As a result, you may not feel comfortable sending sensitive information this way. If you do use e-mail, however, remember that any information sent via this method to parents must also be provided for those families who don't have a computer. Keep in mind that none of these communication methods are time consuming, and they can win friends and influence people when you need parental support.

▶ 3. Ask family members if their child has any special circumstances you need to know about. A child might be in therapy, under the care of a medical doctor, or living with someone other than a parent. Family members may share that there is a divorce happening or that there has been a death in the family. This information can provide clues to children's behavior at school. If family members have not shared this, but you suspect there may be something occurring at home, consider asking. If you aren't comfortable doing so, contact your school social worker who can help.

▶ 4. If you know a child is receiving therapy, ask the parents or guardian for permission to share information with the therapist. Help family members to understand the importance of being able to work with the therapist to assist with positive progress for their child at school. Most likely, you will need a release of information form that your administrator or support staff can provide. This will allow you to discuss the student with the therapist on an ongoing basis.

▶ 5. Finally, do your best to gain the trust of the parents with whom you work. Try to find ways to express concerns or to get information that is not abrasive or blaming. Show your appreciation when it's clear they have made an effort to comply with something you've requested. Express a genuine affection for their child—no matter how long it takes for you to think of something positive to say. Parents and family members who trust you and are at ease will be far more likely to be cooperative and to share important information.

Ongoing Communication

Ongoing communication does not mean calling families three or four times a week to report bad behavior or to complain about a student. Keeping in touch with families in a way that will assure their cooperation should you need it is one important objective of good communication. Look below for some useful suggestions.

▶ 1. It is very true that your first call to families should be a positive one. Make an effort to contact families by phone to introduce yourself. Do this during the first or second week of school after you have formed an impression of your students and can find something positive to say about each one—even if it's that you are glad to see him or her in school every day. If circumstances make it impossible for you to contact family members by phone—after you have made every reasonable effort—be sure to send something written in a positive tone. Then, don't be a stranger—keep the communication going throughout the school year. And remember that parents are eager to hear positive things. So don't forget how important it is to call or write with good news.

▶ 2. As a special education teacher, you will most likely be working with general education teachers who have your students in their classes. You may want to talk with these teachers to decide who will be the one to contact families of the students with disabilities. It is often less confusing for everyone if only one teacher is the contact person, and usually the special education teacher works with the parents of students with special needs. Families should be aware, however, that two teachers are involved in the education of their child and that they can communicate with either or both of them when they desire to do so.

▶ 3. Remember that parents of students with disabilities are important partners with you in the education of their child. Keeping them involved with their child's academic and behavioral progress throughout the school year can increase the possibility of success. Daily or weekly notes home, check-off forms, stickers, and good news certificates are all ways you can help family members keep abreast of their child's academic and behavioral development. Find some way of communicating with your students' family members on a regular basis, and be sure these contacts include a generous amount of positive information whenever possible.

▶ 4. There will no doubt be times when you must contact family members due to academic or behavioral concerns. If you have done a good job of keeping lines of communication open with them, you will probably find them willing to work with you when problems arise. You may need to coordinate rewards or consequences between home and school or ask parents to respond daily to teacher reports that are sent home. If families know and trust you and feel you have the best interests of their child at heart (due to your consistency in communicating with them), they will be more likely to respond positively to your request for their input and help. If they have never heard your voice except to blame or complain, your request for help may elicit a different reaction. Remember also that you will make parent conference time and report card time much more comfortable for yourself, your students, and their parents if parents have been aware on an ongoing basis of any concerns you may have. There should be no real surprises at conference time (or in report cards). If there are continuing concerns, these meetings should provide time for a face-to-face discussion of how things are going and what more can be done, if necessary.

▶ 5. Keep in mind that you may be sharing conference time with a general education teacher, and be sure you are on the same page regarding academic, social, and behavioral concerns before you meet with parents. So confer beforehand to compare notes to assure that you present a united front. Keep notes on all of your parent conferences and on all of the parent contacts you have made throughout the year. You may need to refer back to them if there is a chronic problem with a student. If you have documentation, parents cannot say that they were unaware of your concerns. (Keeping copies of notes home to parents can be important also and are made easy by using carbonless premade parent notes that can be purchased in many teaching supply stores.)

IEP Meetings

IEP meetings can be a daunting experience for some parents, so kindness and sensitivity on the part of all staff members should be the bywords at these meetings. For some ideas on how you can make this a positive experience for families, read on. (Please note that IDEA 2004 allows and encourages the use of alternative ways to hold IEP meetings such as conference calls and video conferencing. Be sure you know your school district's policy in this regard.)

▶ 1.   This meeting can sometimes be difficult for families, whether it is the initial placement meeting, an annual meeting, or a three-year reevaluation. Consider that when they come, they must face the fact that their child has been or might be diagnosed with problems that will affect or are affecting their performance at school and other areas of their life. This can be unsettling for the most optimistic of parents. As the special education teacher and the person who probably has the most contact with family members, consider it your job to help them feel comfortable. Be sure someone in the office knows the family is coming and provides them with a place to wait if they are early. Greet them and, if possible, take a little time to answer any last-minute questions. Be sure they are clear about which other professionals will attend the meeting and why they are there. It would be a nice gesture on your part if you contacted parents before the IEP meeting to find out if there are any special concerns they may want addressed. This phone call can also serve as a friendly reminder of the upcoming meeting.

▶ 2.   Also, be aware that some families may feel intimidated by the group of professionals who may attend the meeting. Most support staff members have had experience working with parents and do their best to make them feel comfortable and welcome. But don't hesitate to question or clarify remarks or statements they make if you think parents may not understand or be confused—sometimes while talking, educators slip into jargon that family members may not understand. If you think this might be the case, find a sensitive way to rephrase the remark or to ask the person who made it to do so.

▶ 3.   The IDEA 2004 legislation has placed emphasis on parental involvement in the IEP process. The IEP should be developed at the meeting and should not be brought as a completed document. One reason for this is to allow family members to have input, and sometimes we as professionals forget this. This is probably one of the most important things for team members to keep in mind throughout the meeting. As the special education teacher, take the responsibility to be sure parents have their say as the IEP is developed. Assuming they have nothing to offer is assuming they know nothing about their own child.

▶ 4.   Take the time to listen to parents. Hopefully, if the team has done its job well, family members will relax and become comfortable enough to share their concerns and other things that may prove very valuable to you in dealing with their child in the classroom. This may also be a time when you can have a productive discussion about classroom or behavior concerns. These kinds of things can then be incorporated into the IEP, and the document will become what it is meant to be—a truly individualized education program for the student.

Parent Conferences

Conference time can be a golden opportunity for you as a special education teacher if you do some thoughtful planning. Many parents whom you might never see otherwise may make an effort to come on that day or evening. It can be your one chance to encourage a good working relationship, discuss an issue face-to-face, or reassure a concerned parent. Collaborating with your general education partner is a must to be able to present the whole picture to family members. Read on to see how you can make the most of this opportunity.

▶ 1. Unless you are in a self-contained classroom (where students with disabilities spend most of their school day), you will need to meet with the general education teacher to plan for conference time. This planning, however, should not begin the week before conferences are scheduled. Early in the school year, you and the general education teacher should decide on such important issues as academic grading, collection of work samples, and documentation of social growth and behavioral issues for the students with disabilities. If this is done well in advance, then planning later in the year for parent conference time should go smoothly. (See Chapter 6, Report Cards and Grading, for more specific ideas.)

▶ 2. As noted above, thoughtful planning is a must. Each student is an individual, and each conference should reflect that. You might want to develop a form for your own use or even to give to the parents at the conclusion of the meeting. It could include such things as a brief comment on progress in academic areas that describes both a strength and an area of need, a comment on behavior and social interaction, and one or two suggestions about how the family could help at home with specific skills the student is working on. Of course, you will expand on each of these areas during the conference. This form can also serve as a way for you and your general education partner to plan. If you make this form something for parents to take home, then they have a written record of what transpired. As a result, you and your general education partner can be more confident that the parents understand your evaluation of their child. Of course, you would encourage parents to call later if questions arise. Most school systems encourage—and some even expect—teachers to gather a compilation of student work that illustrates the student's progress—or lack thereof. This will provide you with evidence to support what you tell parents about how their child is doing academically. Let parents take this work home to share and talk about with their child.

▶ 3. Parent conference time can also be an opportunity to talk about other issues. Personal care concerns are best discussed face-to-face, and this would be a good time to do so. In addition to your general education partner, you might want to ask your school nurse or the social worker to sit in and help with this delicate subject. Conference time is also an appropriate time to discuss behavior and socialization issues. But remember that if some of these things have been ongoing problems, conference time should not be the first time parents hear about them. It is unfair to spring potentially sensitive issues for the first time at conferences. This time should be used to discuss progress and to decide if other courses of action are needed.

▶ 4. It's always a good idea to begin and end the conference with something positive, even if you are only able to begin by saying how glad you are to meet Caroline's parents and end by saying that you are so happy she is in school every day. Starting with a kind word can help family members to be at ease and to be more open to what you have to say. Closing with something nice might help soften any negative parts of the conference so they can leave with the feeling that you care and are working for the best interest of their child.

▶ 5. Most family members are understanding and willing to work with you to help their child succeed even when problems occur. Occasionally, however, you may have people that, for whatever reason, come to the meeting feeling angry, belligerent, or defensive or who may become so as the conference progresses. If you have any reason to think that your meeting with specific parents may not go well, plan ahead. Alert your administrator, and let him or her know of your concern and what time the particular conference is scheduled. See if that person could stand by to make him- or herself available should you need help. You and your general education partner may also want to consider asking another person to attend such as the school social worker or psychologist who may know about the child and the family. If these people are not available, ask another teacher—perhaps someone who has had the child in class in the past. If you are alone in a self-contained classroom, you may want to ask another teacher—or even someone from your building's special education administration—to be with you. In situations like this, it is always a good idea to have a witness. If possible, let the parents or family members know ahead of time that someone else will be at the conference, and if it is someone who has had previous dealings with the child and family, it will not seem unusual. And remember to keep calm. Don't raise your voice or argue. If the parent(s) seems very unreasonable and cannot talk rationally, call your principal. Then tell the parent that you will say no more until the principal has arrived. At this point, your administrator may want to take over the discussion or may invite the family member(s) to finish the conference in his or her office—with or without you. But be sure your principal understands your side of the issue beforehand so he or she can put things in proper perspective.

 Many parents—especially of younger children with disabilities—may enter a conference feeling somewhat apprehensive. Consider beginning by complimenting both parent and child, or by telling something the child has shared with you about something special—or even ordinary—that has happened at home. Also, try to validate efforts parents have made to connect with the school such as emptying backpacks when their child comes home, returning notes promptly, letting you know about something that has happened at home that could affect their child at school, and so forth. These are great ways to help parents relax. Be sure to stress that both you and the parents are working as a team toward the same goal: to help the child be successful in school.

Stating things in the positive as you discuss the child can encourage a willingness on the part of parents to help with problems or concerns. Even something negative can be stated this way. For example, if you say, "Your child has the ability to focus on his or her work," indicates that the child has the ability to do what is expected—and sounds much better than saying, "Your child talks and daydreams rather than completing his or her work." Of course, you need to complete the conversation with a more pointed discussion of how you and the parents can work together to be sure the child accomplishes what he or she has the ability to do.

Documentation

Brain overload is an occupational hazard for all teachers but especially for special education teachers. And this is one good reason to document your communications with parents. Another relates to the ability to provide evidence of your attempts to contact family members. Read on to see why documentation can be vital in some cases.

▶   1.   As you become familiar with your students, there will no doubt be some that will cause you special concern because of ongoing academic or behavioral problems. As a result, you may find that you must contact family members frequently. If this is the case, consider developing a way to briefly document your contacts and attempts at making contacts. Doing this is especially important if you are unable to reach parents a majority of the times that you try. However, remember not to limit your efforts to daytime hours only. Try evenings or in the morning also to be sure you are giving people a chance to answer when they are home.

▶   2.   You can make up a simple phone log form yourself or use the one provided here (Figure 8.1). If you design one of your own, be sure it includes the student's name; the name of the person whom you attempted to contact; the time and date of attempted contact; whether you left a message, the line was busy, there was no answer, or it was disconnected; and so forth. Also include a brief comment if you did reach someone. These are all important items should you need a record of your attempts to reach a parent or family member. If you are unable to make phone contact with family members, try using a written log of some kind that can go back and forth daily with the student between school and home. You can use a spiral notebook of any convenient size and do a day-by-day record of your comments and family members' replies. If there is an agreement between you and the family, most students will not balk at taking the notebook home and bringing it back. Remember that you will want to be sure to include good news whenever you can to foster continued participation on the part of the parents and to encourage the student. The log will provide documentation as to how involved family members are willing to be on behalf of their child.

▶   3.   Whether your information is based on a log of phone conversations or daily written communication sent home to parents, remember that it can provide the facts you need if uninvolved parents seem to feel they haven't been informed about problems or issues regarding their child.

Figure 8.1 School-Family Telephone Log

School-Family Telephone Log

Student _____

Parent _____

Home Phone _____

Parent Work Phone _____

Day	Time	Response	Comments

*Response List:

A. **Spoke with parent**   E. **No adult at home**

B. **Busy signal**   F. **Parent declined to speak**

C. **No answer**   G. **Phone disconnected**

D. **Spoke with relative**   H. **Family initiated call**

Other _____

_____

Source: Jill Lindberg, 2004

Assistance From School Support Staff

Whether or not you have parental backing in dealing with students with behavioral or academic challenges, remember that you are not alone. Support staff members can work with you alone, as well as with involved family members, to find ways to address your concerns. Don't hesitate to call on them. Read on to see how you can enlist their aid.

▶ 1. If you feel additional input would be helpful regarding concerns you have about certain students, don't hesitate to involve support staff. (See Chapter 9, Working With Support Staff, for more information.) Parents should be aware of the additional services that are available to them and their child at your school. If you feel it is appropriate, feel free to provide information about the kinds of services offered by the guidance counselor, psychologist, social worker, and other support staff. Depending on what the policies in your school district allow, you may be able to meet informally with parents and certain support staff and, of course, formally at an IEP review meeting to develop strategies to help the student. Even if parents are not involved for whatever reason, support staff should be available to assist you with your concerns.

▶ 2. The makeup of a support staff often varies from school to school, so be sure you know who is in your building—and get their schedules so you will know when they are there. This staff could include one or more social workers; guidance counselors; psychologists; speech and language, occupational, and physical therapists; and medical professionals such as nurses. Your school could also have others. It's a good idea to introduce yourself to these people, and tell them about your position and your students. In this way, if and when you need their help—with either students or parents—you won't be a stranger.

▶ 3. Be sure to ask what kinds of services these professionals provide in your school. (See Chapter 9, Working With Support Staff, for some of the services these people might be able to provide.) You can request that these staff members meet informally with you and the parents of certain students of concern to offer suggestions and ideas if you feel this might be helpful. So don't hesitate to contact them on behalf of your students.

▶ 4. Most districts have a procedure used by support staff for referring students for formal services. Following this process is vital. Doing otherwise may jeopardize the positive relationship you want to foster with the professionals who provide these services. You might also want advice from support staff members about how you can talk with parents about the concerns that have prompted you to begin a formal referral process.

▶ 5. As the school year progresses, you may find that, despite your best efforts, you have a student or students whose inappropriate behavior is escalating. This might be a good time to consider consulting with one or more support staff members as well as to be sure parents are aware of the situation. Remember, though, that if you have had ongoing communication with parents, this type of concern should not come as a complete surprise. Be sure you have gathered enough evidence, including the varied reward and consequence systems you have used, parent contact and involvement, whole-school discipline procedures, and anything else you have tried. This will show that you have made a good-faith effort to deal with the problem yourself before asking for help from a support-staff member and for more involvement from parents. But remember that you might need to reconvene the IEP team to create a formal behavior plan to deal with serious ongoing problems. Appropriate support-staff members—and parents—should be part of the team to assist you with developing this plan.

Working With Support Staff

T his chapter is full of good news for special education teachers—and it starts with the fact that you are not alone as you work with your students with special education needs. These students often present numerous challenges to their teachers, and other professionals in your school are there to help you meet these challenges. New teachers are sometimes unaware that they can call on these people for assistance. Hopefully, this chapter will help you identify these colleagues and the ways they can be helpful to your students—and you.

Chapter Outline

- The IEP and Support Staff Involvement

- Support From the Special Education Administrative Staff

- Support From the School Psychologist

- Support From the School Social Worker

- Support From the Speech and Language Pathologist

- Other Support Staff

The IEP and Support Staff Involvement

The IEP and its development is not the sole responsibility of the special education teacher. It is legally mandated that information come from a variety of

sources including the general education teacher; parents; and when appropriate, any support staff working with the student. Read on to see how you can be sure to get input from these people.

(The information about school support staff came from the Wisconsin Department of Public Instruction Web site, http://www.dpi.state.wi.us and from the Cooperative Educational Service Agency 7 Web site, http://www.cesa7.k12.wi.us.)

▶ 1. As you look over the IEPs for your students, you may see that other staff members are providing services for them. These services could include speech and language therapy, occupational therapy, physical therapy, psychological services, and others. These professionals will contribute their own goal pages to the IEP. Remember to remind them well in advance of IEP meetings in which they must be involved.

▶ 2. The good news here is that these support staff members can do more for you and your students than just show up at the IEP meetings—so don't be shy about asking for their help. The speech and language therapist may have some suggestions for you about things you can do in your classroom to extend what he or she is teaching. The physical and occupational therapists may identify activities you can do with your students that can help develop skills they are working on. The psychologist may have tips and strategies you can use to develop social skills or to improve behavior. Don't hesitate to take full advantage of the valuable assistance these professionals can give you on behalf of your students.

▶ 3. If you have IEPs that include goals for supplementary services, be sure you communicate on a regular basis with the staff members providing these services. Remember that the IEP should provide a complete picture of the student, and as the keeper of the IEP, you should have a basic understanding of all aspects of this document. As time is usually at a premium for everyone, regular face-to-face conversations may not be practical. But most staff members have their own phones with voice mailboxes or even e-mail that can be used as a vehicle for sharing information. When you come to the IEP meeting, as the special education teacher there should be no surprises for you. Remember that parents look to you as the coordinator of their child's educational program, and though you can't be an expert on everything, you should be able to provide them with basic information on most aspects of this document.

▶ 4. Remember also that the IEP should be developed at the IEP meeting. Although most special education teachers come with suggested goals and objectives, there should be opportunities throughout the meeting for all professionals—and the family members present—to provide input. It is important to consider all contributions. Other staff or family members may have a perspective that could cause you to change your mind about a goal or objective you have developed.

▶ 5. Remember that support-staff members are part of a team of professionals that you should be able to count on for assistance. If you feel reticent about approaching them, remember that you are doing it on behalf of your students, not yourself. Note that if consultation time with any of the support staff is indicated on the IEP, then it is required by law that you meet with them for the designated amount of time to discuss the student's progress.

Support From the Special Education Administrative Staff

These are the special education experts in your building and should be the go-to people for the most accurate information and answers to your questions. Be sure you get to know them, and never hesitate to take advantage of their expertise—particularly when you have questions that may have legal implications.

▶ 1. Titles of these staff will vary, but most districts have people who supervise special education staff and speak for the district regarding special education issues. Someone like this may be in your school on a full-time or part-time basis. These people often provide updates on district policies and sign-off for the district on IEPs. Know who this person is in your school, when he or she is there, and a telephone or extension number.

▶ 2. Supervisors are often very busy, but don't hesitate to ask for their expert advice when you need to. Other special education teachers or even your school administration may be able to help you with many of your questions. But as noted in the introduction to this strategy, if you feel your question or concern may have legal implications of some kind, be sure to contact your supervisor— better to be safe than sorry.

▶ 3. Another important member of the special education administrative team in many school districts is the person who does some of the testing for initial and three-year reevaluation IEPs and chairs those IEP meetings. This person may be called a diagnostic teacher—or your district might use a different title. Usually, this person has thorough working knowledge of the IEP and is up to date on any district additions or changes. If you have any questions or doubts about what you have written, don't hesitate to go to him or her. Relying on your own knowledge or even that of other special education teachers if you are in doubt about something may not be the best course of action. Remember that this person may be full or part time in your building, so be sure you know the diagnostic teacher's schedule as well as a telephone or extension number.

▶ 4. If you have questions for your supervisor or diagnostic teacher that aren't urgent, consider jotting them on an index card or in a small notebook as you think of them. Then make an appointment to talk when the person is in your building, or put your concerns in his or her mailbox together with your phone or extension number. This gives these busy people some options as to how and when they can respond.

Support From the School Psychologist

These professionals can be a gold mine of information and support for special education teachers. You may be pleasantly surprised at some of the services school psychologists can provide for your students. Get to know them, and ask for their valuable advice and suggestions.

▶ 1. School psychologists have specialized training in both psychology and education. They understand how school systems work, the elements of effective teaching, and the components of successful learning. They work with families, teachers, and other school staff to be sure students are able to take full advantage of their educational opportunities. These professionals are also involved in testing students who are referred for special education services.

▶   2.   The psychologist in your school may be full or part time. Be sure you know when he or she is there and how you can contact this person. The psychologist can provide a variety of valuable services to you and your students. He or she can consult with you and the parents of your students about learning and behavior, as well as work with students to evaluate academic skills, socioemotional development, behavior, and eligibility for special education. This person can teach individual students, small groups, and even whole-class lessons about conflict resolution, anger management, social skills, and so on. He or she can offer strategies for learning and behavior management. There may even be a goal page on an IEP of some of your students that relates to psychological services. So you can see that the school psychologist can provide much more than just testing results at an IEP meeting.

▶   3.   You may have students about whom you have serious concerns regarding academics, behavior, or social development that you might not feel equipped to handle alone. You should not feel you are an unsuccessful teacher if you don't have all the answers for the serious problems of some of your students. In fact, it is your responsibility to seek help from a professional who has additional training and experience—and your school psychologist could fill that bill. This person can also be a liaison between school and home and even the doctor's office. Having the additional support of the psychologist can also sometimes help parents realize the seriousness of your concern. Don't hesitate to become familiar with the services this person can offer you.

▶   4.   As noted previously, your school psychologist may be able to provide lessons about social skills, anger management, conflict resolution, or other similar issues you may feel would benefit your students. If your students are in a general education classroom, consult with the general education teacher to see if something like this could be presented. Even though the psychologist may not previously have done classroom teaching in your school, don't hesitate to ask about this if it is a service you would like. Together with the general education teacher, you may be able to develop a time schedule and some lesson ideas—and students always enjoy having someone else come in to be their teacher.

Support From the School Social Worker

You may or may not be aware of all of the valuable services your school social worker can provide for you and your students. These people have specialized training in crisis intervention and in working with families—two areas that can be of real concern for teachers. So here is another resource to assist you in areas in which you may feel you need help.

▶   1.   Your school social worker is an integral link between school, home, and your community. He or she works in collaboration with school personnel as a bridge for communication in these areas. Sometimes a family situation is so delicate that it may be uncomfortable for you to handle it alone. In this case, your school social worker could be a good person to call on. This person has special training in crisis intervention and can help you deal with family members in a sensitive and appropriate manner. The social worker can also help parents access services from agencies and community organizations that can be of assistance to them. He or she can help families with paperwork and insurance concerns and can even locate an interpreter if needed.

▶ 2.   Another important service your school social worker can provide is to assist with early identification and prevention of problems in school—another area in which this person's training in crisis intervention is crucial. The social worker can work with students who exhibit signs of socioemotional, physical, or behavioral difficulties that are interfering with their school adjustment and achievement. This person is another resource in helping students—individually or in groups—to better understand themselves and others, improve relationships, build self-esteem, cope with stress, and develop self-discipline.

▶ 3.   The social worker may also be a good person to call on to assist parents in preparing for an IEP meeting. Sometimes family members of students with special education needs are confused and worried about the fact that their child is in a special education setting for all or part of the school day. They may be concerned about the implications of an IEP and how it will affect their child's future. Your social worker may be able to collaborate with you to help alleviate some of these concerns. He or she may be willing to attend the IEP meeting to help the family members understand the proceedings.

▶ 4.   Special education teachers sometimes find that they must deal with an array of serious student and family concerns. Remember that your school social worker can be a real ally when you must deal with sensitive student or family situations and will do home visits to speak to parents when an issue warrants. Take the time to talk with this person to find out more about the services he or she can provide for you and your students.

Support From the Speech and Language Pathologist

The speech and language pathologist can be of help to you as well as to your students. Strategies taught by this person might potentially be implemented in your classroom or group setting and will help your students function better in school. Be sure to stay informed about what your students are learning with this person.

▶ 1.   The speech and language pathologist in your school is a professional who specializes in speech and communication development and disorders. This person provides services for children who may have difficulty with communication skills that hinder their performance in reading, writing, listening, or speaking. General education students as well as students with special education needs may need services from this person. You may find some speech and language goal pages in the IEPs of some of your students.

▶ 2.   Students with special education needs who are receiving services from the speech and language pathologist may get this help in your classroom or in a resource setting. You may want to talk with this person about having some of the service time in the classroom or in your group setting so that you can better understand what kind of speech or language help your student is receiving. This will enable you to assist the student in learning and practicing the skill(s) in your group or classroom setting.

▶ 3. Know when the speech and language pathologist is in your school—he or she may be full or part time in your building. In addition to providing formal services to students, this person can be a resource for you in helping students who have not been formally identified as needing help with speech or language.

Other Support Staff

In addition to the support staff previously discussed, there may be others in your school who are there to assist your students. These could include an occupational or physical therapist and a school nurse. There may be others in your building as well. As the special education teacher, you may have students receiving services from some of them. Remember that these people are also part of the team that is in place to help you if needed.

▶ 1. Occupational and physical therapists work on helping students improve both fine and gross motor skills. They may do this in your classroom or in another place in your school. Keep in mind that the things they work on are directly related to the student's performance in school, so it's a good idea to be aware of the goals they have for him or her. For example, hand and finger dexterity are important for writing and printing, among other school-related activities. Talk with the occupational therapist about these or other fine motor skills that may be targeted for your student, and ask about ways you can help the student practice them in your classroom or group. Large-muscle activities are usually the domain of the physical therapist. Again, talk with this person to find out if you can work on any kind of large-muscle activities with your student in class or in your group. Remember that what these people teach is directly related to the student's success in your class or group. So helping your student with some of these skills may ultimately enable him or her to be more successful with the things you are teaching.

▶ 2. Remember that you can also use the occupational and physical therapists as resource people. You may have students who do not qualify for their services but who could benefit from tips these professionals could offer you. So get to know them, even if they are not servicing any of your students with special education needs. Find out when they are in your building. Contact them via e-mail, phone, or a note in their mailbox to save their time and yours—and keep your questions brief and to the point. Make it easy for them to provide information for you.

▶ 3. The school nurse is becoming a more frequent fixture in schools, and some schools even have clinics that service the surrounding community. We are sometimes faced with students who are poorly nourished, have chronic health problems, or may occasionally come to school when they are sick and should be home. All teachers should be sensitive to and aware of the physical health of their students, as this can directly affect their performance in school. Below are some ways a school nurse may be able to help with your students.

    a. The school nurse can be a valuable resource for you in several ways. So introduce yourself, and be sure you know when this person is in your building. If you have serious concerns that the health needs of a student are not being met, and you are uncomfortable with approaching family members, call on your school nurse. This person can be a liaison between you and the family, and it is possible that family members will be more open to hearing about these concerns from him or her. Also, be sure to check your students' IEPs to see if nursing services are required due to existing health problems. Students who have diabetes, seizures, asthma, or other serious health issues may have nursing services written directly into their IEP, making it mandatory for you to meet with the nurse to address these issues. Often, there are formal medical plans written by the nurse addressing the procedures to follow in dealing with these medical problems. A copy of this plan should be with the student's IEP—and with the general education teacher if the student spends any time in his or her classroom.

    b. You may be able to use the school nurse as a resource in dealing with sensitive personal-care-related issues. If you are uncomfortable contacting family members in this regard, the nurse may be willing to be the liaison person. Your nurse might even be willing to come to your class or group to talk about nutrition, personal care, and other issues affecting growing children. Don't hesitate to find out about the valuable services this person can provide.

10

Working With Teacher Assistants

"**B**ut I never took a class on how to work with and direct another adult!" If that was your first thought when you were assigned a teacher assistant, take heart. (Please note that titles for persons assisting teachers in their classrooms may be different in your school district. They will be referred to as teacher assistants or assistants in this chapter.) Kindness, respect, and a willingness to work together will go a long way in making this partnership a success. But you must be organized and have a game plan as you think about how your assistant can work with you for maximum benefit to your students. Consider the strategies below as you think about your approach to working with a teacher assistant.

Chapter Outline

- Making a Schedule
- Communication
- Presenting a United Front
- Assigning Responsibilities
- Discussing Concerns

Making a Schedule

If you are one of the fortunate few who has a teacher assistant, you know you have a responsibility to gain the maximum benefit from this help. Developing a schedule is one way to assure this will happen.

▶ 1. It is important that you know what the expectations are in your school system as to how a teacher assistant can be used. There may be some limitations regarding what noncertified personnel can do, or there may be union restrictions. Check with your administrator or your union representative before you decide how you will use your assistant.

▶ 2. Once you are clear as to what your assistant can do with your students, you are ready to develop a schedule. It's critical that you involve this person in this task for several reasons. You want the assistant to be invested in what he or she is doing and to feel that he or she has an opportunity for input. In addition, a mutually planned schedule will help assure there is no misunderstanding as to your expectations of your assistant. Also, be sure that person has some knowledge about and understanding of IEPs—taking a little time to provide this is another way to help your assistant feel invested in supporting your students in reaching their IEP goals. You might even consider providing this person with a copy of the IEP snapshots.

▶ 3. Despite the fact that you have a schedule for your assistant, there will certainly be times when your administrator will need that person for another purpose. Be sure your classroom or group(s) can still function. In other words, have a backup plan. Think about how you can work around the situation and still provide appropriate academic lessons for your students. Create your backup plan as soon as you have your assistant's schedule developed—failing to do so will surely leave you in distress when the inevitable happens.

▶ 4. As the year progresses, you should monitor how well your assistant's schedule is working. Again, asking for input from him or her may provide insight you don't have or suggestions that would be valuable. If you find your assistant is not self-directed or for whatever reason has difficulty following the schedule, be sure to address the issue. Ignoring this can cause a breakdown in your class structure and tension that could affect your students.

▶ 5. Remember to continue the expectations of your assistant throughout the school year, to follow the schedule you have both planned. Together, your goal should be to provide the best possible learning environment for your students. You can set a good example for your teacher assistant by being consistent in following your own schedule on a daily basis.

Communication

Never thought of yourself as "The Great Communicator?" Being able to communicate well with your teacher assistant can be crucial to the success of your partnership. And the success of this partnership can be crucial to your students' success—which should be the ultimate goal for both of you.

▶ 1. Working to make sure your assistant is invested in the success of your students should be your main goal. Involve this person in student-centered activities—not just copying materials and doing errands. This means you need to make it clear that you are willing, as far as possible, to include this person in the planning and execution of your lessons. If your assistant will be teaching a certain type of lesson on a regular basis, you may want to model for him or her to be sure your expectations are understood. Remember to compliment and recognize success and appropriate initiative on the part of your assistant. The regular use of the words *please* and *thank you* go a long way in building respect and also provide a good model for your students.

▶ 2. Be willing to share the affection of your students. Don't feel threatened if they relate well to your assistant. You may find he or she can work successfully with someone you might find difficult—and you may truly value this person's success with that student. Communicate your appreciation of his or her achievements—another way for your assistant to feel invested in you and your efforts with your class.

▶ 3. A successful relationship with your teacher assistant means you will need to be able to communicate when things are not going well. It's always best to confront small issues before they become big ones and get out of hand. Find a way to discuss your concerns in a friendly way without blaming anyone. Come to a definite agreement as to how you both will handle the situation in the future—don't be ambiguous about what will be done.

▶ 4. Sad to say, sometimes, despite your best efforts and intentions, there may be difficulties with your assistant. First of all, realize that you are not the only teacher to experience this. Just because you are placed in a room with someone does not necessarily mean things will work out perfectly. Your administrator will, of course, expect you to make every effort to deal with your concerns before he or she becomes involved. As you work to resolve your difficulties, you may want to document what you have tried and the conversations you have had with your assistant. Then, should you or someone else need this information, you won't have to depend on your memory.

▶ 5. Finally, remember that the primary reason you have an assistant is to provide help to your students—but be sure this person isn't doing too much. He or she should not be doing the work for your students, and you need to communicate that.

Presenting a United Front

"A house divided against itself cannot stand," Abraham Lincoln once said. This applies to you and your assistant as you work with your students. Presenting a united front is very important because students will recognize and capitalize upon obvious differences and tensions.

▶ 1. It is imperative that you and your assistant present a united front to your class or group. A dangerous precedent will be set if your students think they can play one of you against the other. The job of both you and your assistant is to provide an appropriate academic, social, and behavioral atmosphere for your students. This can best be done if you can agree to manage these three areas as a team.

▶ 2. One of the best ways to assure that you and your assistant are united in your efforts to educate your students is to make this person feel like a contributing and productive member of your teaching team. In addition to including your assistant in your planning and teaching, your students should be expected to treat this person with the same respect and deference with which they treat you. This can only happen if you make the expectation clear through your own actions and words.

▶ 3. Sometimes teaching teams fall into the trap of vying for the affection of the students. You and your assistant are not in a popularity contest. View your relationship as that of two people having different things to offer to both the teaching situation and the students. Make an effort to recognize and appreciate what your assistant brings to your classroom and to your students—and stop to recognize and appreciate what you contribute also.

▶ 4. You and your assistant need to be united about many things as you work together—but none more so than behavior management. Of course, you will have a behavior management program in place for your class or group, and you need to make sure your assistant understands your procedures. Your students should know they won't be able to play one of you against the other—that when one of you makes a decision, they cannot go to the other for a different outcome.

▶ 5. If you become concerned that your assistant is not on the same page as you and seems unwilling to support your classroom procedures and rules, address the issue. But find a way to do so without blaming. Consider reviewing the procedures and rules, and ask for input from this person. This is another way of helping him or her to feel invested in what you are trying to accomplish with your students. Don't ignore a situation like this because it will cause tension and discomfort—and your students will be aware of what is happening and may try to capitalize on the circumstances.

Assigning Responsibilities

Do you think of your assistant as the queen (or king) of the copying machine? If this is the sum total of your job description for this person, you aren't using this wonderful resource to its fullest. Rethink your views, and begin adding a new dimension to your classroom or teaching situation.

▶ 1. Don't ignore this very important part of working with an assistant. Assuming that he or she will know what to do or can anticipate your needs or those of your students may have unfortunate consequences. Before you sit down with your assistant to discuss responsibilities (yes, it's important to include this person in planning the use of him or her), be sure you have a clear idea of the kind of things you would like him or her to do. This should include responsibilities with students as well as clerical work for you.

▶ 2. Talk with your assistant about any particular areas of strength or interest he or she may have that could benefit your students. If these can be utilized in your classroom or with your group, be sure to do so. But remember, you are the teacher and in charge of your students' educational experiences. Ultimately, it is your decision as to which responsibilities you will assign your assistant.

▶ 3. Once you have decided on the division of labor in your classroom or group, it's also your responsibility to monitor the work your assistant does—especially with your students. Be sure you are clear and specific as to your assignment for this person. As time goes on, you may find that your assistant is self-directed and knows what to do with minimal instruction from you. But even under these circumstances, you still need to be sure appropriate educational practices are being implemented.

▶ 4. If responsibilities include work outside the classroom—whether clerical work for you or helping your students—you need to be aware of time spent on these projects. Most people have a good work ethic and will be aware of their time-related responsibilities to you and your students. But if you find your assistant disappearing for long periods of unaccounted-for time, you may need to tighten up his or her schedule.

▶ 5. Remember that making good use of your teacher assistant can double the educational effectiveness in your classroom. This can be especially important when you are working with students with special education needs, as they often require a good deal of individual attention. This reason alone should motivate any good teacher to be sure time spent with a teacher assistant is used to the maximum benefit for the students.

Discussing Concerns

Every relationship encounters a bump in the road now and then—including relationships in a classroom. If you have worked to develop a respectful and cordial partnership with your assistant by implementing some of the strategies in this chapter, it may be easier to get things back on track. Here are some additional ideas to consider if you conclude it's time to address a concern.

▶ 1. The most important thing to remember is to address an issue early on. Don't wait and hope it will go away. It's much easier to nip something in the bud than to let it become a long-term habit. If you take care of things right away, it may just take a few minutes of friendly conversation rather than a long, tense discussion that could end with hard feelings. Remember, too, that tension in your classroom or group can be detrimental to your students, who usually know when something is wrong.

▶ 2. Another important thing to remember is to organize your thoughts, and be sure you have some examples of the situation that is causing you concern. Also, think about how you will approach the issue. Don't blame or use words like *always* and *never.* Listen calmly to what the other person has to say. Ask for input and ideas as to how you can both work to solve the problem.

▶ 3. If your assistant seems upset or angry or refuses to acknowledge at least part of the responsibility for your concern, you may want to get some help. First, try someone in the building whom you trust and feel you can talk to—perhaps another teacher or support-staff member. Someone else may have a different perspective or an idea you haven't thought of. Don't go to your administrator immediately because he or she will expect you to do everything possible to solve the problem yourself first.

▶ 4. If difficulties persist, remember that it may be helpful to document examples of your concerns as well as the things you have done to address them. You don't need a long narrative—just sequential notes so you don't have to rely only on your memory. If you have gotten to this point, it may be time to meet with your administrator. If you decide to do this, remember to present the facts without blaming and to indicate your concern for the welfare of your students. At this point, hopefully, your administrator will take the lead in assisting you in solving the problem.

11

Working With Administration

Having a successful relationship with your school principal is very important for you and for your students with special education needs. Some administrators have had limited experience in working with these students, and some have had a great deal of exposure. Whatever the case, you are still the first and best advocate for your students and will want to have a positive relationship with your principal for your students' sake as well as your own.

Chapter Outline

- Understanding Your Principal's View of Special Education in Your School
- Communicating With Your Principal
- Principal Observations and Evaluations
- Professional Development
- What Is a Professional Learning Community?

Understanding Your Principal's View of Special Education in Your School

Some principals are less than enthusiastic about having students with special education needs in their school. And sad to say, some of the reasons for this attitude can be laid at the feet of the special education staff. Make up your mind that your professionalism, positive perspective, and dedication to educating

your students will impress your principal and help to put a positive spin on special education for him or her.

▶ 1. If you are new in a school, it probably won't take you too long to find out how special education is viewed there. Sometimes this opinion is filtered down from the principal to teachers and other staff members. If you feel there is resistance within your school for whatever reason, decide you will do your best to help change it. Below are some nonthreatening ways to begin making that change that will send your principal a positive message about your professional commitment.

    a. Stick to your schedule—don't cancel your groups unless you have a good reason.

    b. Keep the general education teachers up to date with important information about your students.

    c. Be willing to include in your groups some students from the general education classroom who may benefit from your help, and assist these students as well as your students with disabilities when you are involved in whole-group activities.

    d. Offer to go on field trips that include your students.

    e. Be sure your paperwork is accurate and up to date.

    f. Keep your administrator apprised of any serious concerns regarding your students.

▶ 2. Special education has undergone many transformations over the years, and there may still be principals who are not aware of all the latest legal and philosophical changes. It's up to special education administration and staff to help get them up to speed. Most school districts are now including students with special education needs in the general education classroom to varying degrees when appropriate, rather than keeping them in self-contained classrooms. Some principals have difficulty making the shift in thinking from the old idea of self-contained special education classrooms to inclusive general education classrooms. As you assess your school situation, think about what your principal's philosophy might be. Special education administration or staff in your building may be able to help you with this. However, remember to separate fact from opinion as you listen to what they have to say.

▶ 3. Another way to find out how your principal views special education in your school is to ask. However, don't stop him or her in the hallway for a philosophical discussion. Make an appointment—and indicate what you want to address when you do so. That way your principal will be better prepared to talk with you.

▶ 4. If you are concerned about the philosophy of special education in your school and feel changes are needed, remember that you need to work along with, not against, the principal and your colleagues to help make this happen. If you are a new teacher, the best thing you can do is to demonstrate the dedication you have to your students through your professionalism and commitment to your responsibilities. As you become a respected educator in the eyes of your principal and other staff members, your ability to advocate for and implement change will grow.

Communicating With Your Principal

New teachers—and sometimes even veteran educators—might feel uncomfortable with or intimidated by their principal. But working to keep lines of communication open with your administrator can help alleviate some of these feelings. And you can begin to do this in a way that is nonthreatening to you. Think about some of the suggestions below.

▶ 1. Consider a newsletter. The main audience for this, of course, would be parents and family members, but slipping a copy in your principal's mailbox is one sure way of letting him or her know what's happening in your classroom or with your small groups. If you feel overwhelmed with responsibilities, think biweekly or monthly—it doesn't have to be a weekly effort. Include in the newsletter such things as special activities or projects, a list of students who have been faithful in submitting homework, field trips, new skills being introduced, tips to help family members support learning at home, and so on. You could even include a section written by students. All of these things are positive indicators of your efforts and progress with your students—something your principal will be glad to know about. So in this way, you can communicate with your administrator and not even set foot in his or her office if that makes you feel uncomfortable.

▶ 2. Communicate with your principal to keep him or her informed about any escalating behavior situations with your students. If, despite your best efforts—including various rewards and consequences, parent contact, and consultation with support staff—you continue to have serious concerns about a student, tell your principal. He or she will not want to get a call from an irate parent or have a serious behavior incident occur at school without being forewarned of this possibility. You can be sure this kind of communication will be very much appreciated.

▶ 3. Feel comfortable to stop your principal in the hall to briefly give him or her some good news about a student who may have academic or behavior difficulties. But remember not to engage in a long conversation—you are both busy. This could be an icebreaker for you and a way to begin to feel comfortable about approaching him or her. In addition, you might consider inviting your principal to stop by to see a special activity or project involving your students. Your own open-door policy sends a positive message about what you are doing with your students.

▶ 4. If you do your best to hold your groups, collaborate with colleagues, attend to concerns you have with your students, and execute your paperwork correctly and in a timely manner, you send your principal the message that you are an asset to the special education staff and the school as a whole. This is one of the most important messages you can communicate.

▶ 5. If you are able to do some of the things suggested in this strategy, you will probably feel more comfortable with your principal. You may even be ready to approach him or her with new ideas or changes that would have a positive effect on your students. But remember that unless your administrator has an open-door policy, you need to make an appointment to talk. Be courteous, let him or her know what you want to discuss ahead of time, come with an agenda, and don't overstay your welcome—again, remember that both of you are busy. But if you have an urgent concern, don't wait—let your principal know that you need to talk as soon as possible. No principal wants to be surprised by a serious issue with a student or family member that has gone too far.

Principal Observations and Evaluations

Observations and evaluations by the principal can strike fear into the heart of the most seasoned teacher. But there are some things you can do well before your administrator sets a date to visit your classroom or group that will help minimize the trepidation you feel. Read on for ideas to help calm your nerves.

▶ 1. It goes without saying that you should strive to have your day-to-day teaching be of the highest quality. You should not be putting on a show of good teaching only on the day your administrator observes you. If you are in the habit of regularly making lesson plans, preparing thoroughly ahead of time, and evaluating what you have taught based on your students' progress, then you should be ready to be observed.

▶ 2. You should be able to get a copy of the evaluation form ahead of time. Do so, look it over, and identify strengths and areas of your teaching that need improvement. Then you can begin to work on things that you need to rectify.

▶ 3. Ask the principal to come to observe you informally. But if you are recoiling in horror at this suggestion, consider the following idea. Get comfortable being observed by asking a fellow teacher, support staff member, or special education administrator to come and watch you teach. You might want to start with a trusted colleague with whom you feel comfortable. Then, work your way up to people with whom you are less familiar. This will help both you and your students become accustomed to having a visitor in your classroom or to your group. Be sure, however, that you clear this with your administrator, especially if your observer must leave his or her teaching duties to help you.

▶ 4. Remember that the purpose of having someone watch you teach—beyond helping you and your students become comfortable with an observer—is to ask for constructive criticism. Be open to doing so. Then, if you feel the criticism is valid, make changes or improvements. Be sure to ask your observer to comment on areas you have identified on the evaluation form as things you want to improve. If you have become comfortable with being observed by colleagues, you may be ready to ask your principal to do an informal observation or just to stop in from time to time and watch all or part of a lesson. Ask for feedback, and accept criticism graciously. If possible, implement any suggestions your administrator gives you.

▶ 5. If you feel the need to discuss your evaluation with your principal, be sure to make an appointment to do so. If you disagree with something, do so professionally. Don't whine or make excuses. Usually, there is a place on the evaluation form where you can write your own comments. Again, so do in a professional way. If you have serious concerns about your evaluation that cannot be resolved by meeting with your administrator, you may have the option of seeking assistance from the teachers' union in your district. But this should be a last resort. It is in your very best interest to try to resolve disagreements of this kind at the school level if at all possible. Involving outside assistance can sometimes create tension between a teacher and administration.

Professional Development

Special education teachers today have to contend with constant changes in their field. New ways to teach, new criteria for disabilities, changes in documentation—these are all things that face special educators on an ongoing basis. Although keeping abreast of these changes can be a challenge, your principal will expect you to do so. Here are some ideas that can help.

▶ 1. Professional development can take place in your school, within your school district, or out of the district. Find out from your principal how information about these opportunities is disseminated in your school. Speak with your special education administrator to be sure you are on a list to receive notices of any workshops or inservices in your field—especially those dealing with changes in documentation requirements or service delivery for your district.

▶ 2. Your school may be a Professional Learning Community (PLC)—ask your principal or fellow teachers. The major focus of a PLC is to ensure high levels of learning for all students. A second focus is on the continual learning of teachers. The culture of the PLC school developed by the staff and administration is one of collaboration rather than teacher isolation. See the information following this strategy under the heading, What Is a PLC?

▶ 3. Professional development can be as close as another teacher's classroom in your building. Ask your principal if you can observe a colleague for curriculum or management ideas. Look for someone in your building who has a strength in an area where you feel you need help. If you're not sure, ask the principal or another teacher to recommend someone for you to observe. Meet with that person beforehand to discuss what you will see, and then find time after the observation to discuss and corroborate what you saw. In addition, curriculum meetings, special education policy and procedure meetings, grade-level meetings, and collaborative support teams for students who have academic or behavior needs are all opportunities for teachers to work together to share knowledge, ideas, and skills.

▶ 4. Frequently, school districts offer inservices for all teachers and some specifically for special education teachers. They can deal with documentation, curriculum, classroom management, technology, and more. In addition to the knowledge you gain from these meetings, you can also benefit from connecting with other special educators in your district. Often, the inservice presenters can help you find information and materials or even put you in touch with other teachers who are working in situations similar to yours. Conferences and inservices from outside the district can also be informative. Usually there is a cost for attending, and often it is substantial, so be sure you talk with your principal to see if funds are available through your school before you register. You could incur a significant personal financial expense if you fail to do so.

▶ 5. When making a request to your principal to attend an inservice, conference, or workshop, be sure to ask well in advance so any needed preparations can be made. Arrangements for a substitute may be necessary, you might have to submit a formal written request to attend, and there may be other procedures before things are finalized. Check with your principal to see exactly what is needed. Failing to follow the correct procedure could spell disaster for you and cause consternation for your principal on inservice day.

What Is a Professional Learning Community?

Professional Learning Communities have recently gained acceptance as a reform tool for schools in many parts of the country. The basic assumption of a PLC is that a school exists not only to teach students, but also to ensure that they learn. The shift is from teaching to learning and to finding ways of identifying whether learning is happening for all students. PLCs must consider what students should be learning, how teachers will know if students are learning, and what they will do if some students are having problems learning.

Two important issues for schools that become PLCs are to recognize when students are having difficulty learning and to develop specific ways to assure they succeed in the future. Schools that are PLCs are required to identify these students quickly and to intervene immediately rather than rely on remediation. Identifying data should be based on formative or ongoing assessment rather than summative assessment such as state-mandated tests. These schools are also expected to make it mandatory for these students to spend extra time working on targeted skills and to receive additional help until they master the target skills or concepts taken from the formative data.

Teachers in schools that are PLCs are also obliged to collaborate to ensure student success. Collaboration, a key word for PLCs, is defined as educators working in teams to evaluate and improve their classroom practices. The success of PLCs is based on results. Teachers work together to determine the current level of student achievement, establish a goal for improvement, and work toward that goal. Finally, they must be able to show periodic evidence of success.

Schools that become PLCs are obligated to assure that all students learn, and the success of this program depends on the commitment and persistence of the educators themselves.

12

Working Within Your School Community

"No man is an island" is a quote that rings especially true in a school setting. Gone are the days when teachers close their doors and teach in isolation. This is particularly true for special educators. To help create the best possible learning environment for students with special education needs, it's up to us as teachers to pave the way by becoming full partners in the school community with our general education colleagues and other staff members. Read on for some tips on how to make this all-important partnership happen.

Chapter Outline

- Becoming Part of the Team
- Teacher Buddies and Mentors
- To Socialize or Not to Socialize
- The Teachers' Room
- Ask for Help, Offer to Help
- Other Supports for New Teachers

Becoming Part of the Team

Becoming a respected part of a school staff is especially important for special education teachers. Often, for reasons made clear in this strategy, special education

teachers need to make an extra effort. Here are some sure-fire suggestions that can help accomplish that very important goal.

▶ 1. Special education teachers are like the new kid on the block—it seems we have to work harder at proving ourselves before we belong. How can you do this while still maintaining your integrity? If you are new in a school or are in a school with lots of new teachers, there are some things you can do to help ensure that you become a valued team member. One of the best ways is to avoid the gossip mill. Don't get involved in school rumors and idle talk. Avoid becoming known as someone who spreads things about colleagues or students—true or untrue. Find trusted friends; be a trusted friend.

▶ 2. The Teachers' Room has a reputation—deserved or undeserved. Should you spend your lunchtime there? What are the pitfalls, if any? This room sometimes becomes the repository for all the gripes and complaints teachers have about each other, the principal, parents, students, and almost anyone else in the line of fire. Daily lunches there can sometimes weigh you down with information you don't need or want. Or you may find yourself feeling compelled to share something uncomfortable—especially about your students. Consider these things, and visit occasionally. Maybe lunch alone or with those trusted friends isn't such a bad idea. (See this chapter, To Socialize or Not to Socialize and The Teachers' Room, for more considerations.)

▶ 3. Do consider, however, that eating in the teachers' room provides you with an opportunity to speak to general education teachers about students with special education needs that they might have in their class. You can also share lunch in your classroom or another comfortable setting—just remember to be professional in your discussion and avoid gossip or complaints.

▶ 4. Be a team player. Offer to join a committee or two. Once on the committee, volunteer for a job you feel capable of doing. Participate in at least some optional or volunteer school activities. Show up, and stay till the end. Smile—even if you don't feel like it. Don't complain about school activities, policies, and goings-on—you never know who may be listening.

▶ 5. Some feel that special education teachers are the ones with "just those few kids, who don't have to do all those report cards or have all those papers to correct and who have all that extra time to do those IEPs." We need to prove our worth. Here are some great ways to do that: Follow your schedule every day. Don't be known as someone who cancels for no good reason. Offer to help with field trips; work with students from the general education classroom who could benefit from some extra teacher time. Don't be a wallflower in the general education classroom. Establish yourself as a bona fide teacher—not a teacher assistant. Be an effective disciplinarian with your own students as well as students from the general education classroom. Be a force within your school. See to it that students in addition to your own respect you and listen to you. Support other teachers' decisions. Ignore those who are special education bashers. Work hard—prove them wrong.

Teacher Buddies and Mentors

If you had one wish as a teacher, what would it be? Many of us would say we'd like another experienced and empathetic educator to confide in—someone who

would take time to help and never make light of any question, no matter how basic. If you do have a buddy teacher or mentor, read on for some ways to nurture the relationship. If someone like that isn't assigned to you, look below for suggestions on how to find that person yourself.

▶ 1. Some schools and school systems have a buddy teacher or mentor teacher in place for staff members who are new. (Some systems have full-time mentors, but many have experienced teachers who mentor as part of their teaching responsibilities.) If you are fortunate enough to have someone like this, here are a few hints to make sure your relationship with that person flourishes.

    a. Be the first to introduce yourself at a time when your buddy or mentor is not busy. Then see if you can set aside a time that is convenient (especially for him or her) when you can regularly meet to talk.

    b. Respect your new friend by coming to your meeting on time and with specific questions you have jotted down—and keep your discussion to school-related topics as well as short and to the point. Your friend may be a classroom teacher, too, and have responsibilities to attend to before or after your meeting.

    c. Don't complain and gossip during your time to talk. Doing so could put this person—whom you hope to make your ally—in an awkward position. Give your buddy feedback. Make use of this person's suggestions and ideas, and let him or her know what worked. Thank your buddy for his or her input. Share something new you've discovered that you think might interest this person. If there is something you can offer your buddy teacher, do so. Perhaps you could share materials such as activity books, games, puzzles, or other things you have purchased for your students. Be sure to look for small ways throughout the school year to show your appreciation for your buddy's kindness—a favorite candy bar, soda, or snack as an occasional surprise would be welcomed by most. Remember that this person is taking time out of his or her day to help you. Your willingness to be considerate, respectful, and appreciative could ultimately earn you a trusted friend.

▶ 2. If your school has no one in place to act as a buddy or mentor for new staff members, there are some things you can do to find one. Learn who the other special education teachers are. You may be able to connect with the person who had your students last year. This would be a good starting point for information and help. If you are the only special education teacher in your school, you may want to connect with one of the general education teachers who works with some of your students. In addition, many school districts allow teachers some time to visit and observe classes in other schools. Take advantage of this opportunity if it is offered—you might make a new friend.

▶ 3. Be honest with the teacher with whom you are trying to make a connection. Tell the person you have questions and concerns and would like someone to act as a sounding board on a regular basis. Ask if he or she would be willing, but don't be angry or upset if the person feels unable to help you—some people, for whatever reason, are uncomfortable in a mentoring position. If you find a willing person, be sure to follow the suggestions in Step 1 of this strategy to assure your relationship stays in good order.

▶ 4. Often, new special education teachers need help and guidance with the heavy load of paperwork responsibilities they have. Some of this paperwork is composed of legal documents that could be used in court, so it is very important that it be done in compliance with district and state regulations and laws. If you have questions about how to complete these documents, be sure to seek out someone who can give you accurate information. Your mentor or buddy teacher may or may not be that person. If you are unsure if you are getting correct information, seek out advice from a special education administrative person in your building.

To Socialize or Not to Socialize

Socializing can have a number of connotations in a school setting—some of them not so positive. Sometimes it is equated with gossiping or spending too much time standing in the hall talking, oblivious to the student chaos around you. On the other hand, getting to know your fellow teachers in a friendly and appropriate way is important. Striking a balance is the trick.

▶ 1. As previously discussed, special education teachers sometimes need to prove their worth to other staff members, and often the way your colleagues view you is the way they view your students with special education needs. So you need to be the goodwill ambassador—for both yourself and your students—and the best way to do that is to build a positive reputation. Remember the suggestions in Chapter 11, Communicating With Your Principal, that will help your administrator view you as a committed professional? Look them over again; they bear repeating. These tips are sure-fire ways to gain support and respect from your colleagues as well.

▶ 2. Remember that you can be cordial and pleasant without being a social butterfly. Greet your colleagues with a kind word and a friendly smile—no matter how you are feeling. Respond to requests, questions, or concerns from other teachers in a gracious manner. Be a team player—join a committee or two, or volunteer for something. Work to be viewed as a welcome addition to your school's staff because of your attitude as well as your professional skills.

▶ 3. As you establish yourself as a respected person in your school, you will become comfortable finding appropriate ways to socialize with others. Those teachers who have the same professional philosophy as you do will gravitate toward you, and you will develop a circle of trusted friends. As you work in your school and observe its culture and dynamics, you will find out where you fit—and the group of teachers with whom you are comfortable. You will be able to make decisions as to how and where you spend your precious free time during the school day. Then you can decide for yourself what part socializing will play in your school day.

The Teachers' Room

An important place in every school, the teachers' room can be a place to escape for a few minutes of solace—to have a quiet lunch or just to take a deep breath.

But it can also be a hotbed of gossip and complaints. It's up to you to decide if and when you want to spend time there. Consider some of the following as you make up your mind.

▶ 1. Inevitably, you will need to decide where you want to spend your lunchtime and those precious few free moments, and the teachers' room may seem to be the logical choice. Here are some things to think about as you make your way there: If you enjoy socializing, consider that the definition of this word as it might apply to the teachers' room could be gossiping or griping. This could include grumbling about other staff members, the principal. a parent or student, or how things are done at your school. So if you decide to go, observe and listen during your first few visits. Then decide what the definition of socializing is in your school and whether or not you want to be part of it.

▶ 2. If grumbling and complaining are a regular part of the dynamics of your teachers' room, you may want to find another place to go. This kind of dialogue can be disillusioning and distressing—especially for newcomers to a school. One of your goals as a new teacher should be to make up your own mind in an objective fashion about other teachers, your principal, the students, and parents. Give yourself time to do this before you listen to others' opinions.

▶ 3. All educators need time to themselves, and it is important that new teachers take some time to regroup during the school day. Usually, the lunch hour provides this opportunity. If the teachers' room doesn't work for you, consider staying in your own room, eating lunch with another teacher, taking a walk, or even buying lunch at a fast food restaurant occasionally. Teaching can be very intense, so don't underestimate the need to get away—and remember that you have several options.

▶ 4. Sometimes the teachers' room gripe sessions extend out into the hallways and to groups of teachers who gather to gossip there. It's usually wise to avoid involvement. You will want to be identified by your principal and other teachers as someone who is professional and who takes his or her responsibilities seriously. Gabbing while students in the hall may need monitoring or while they are alone in the classroom doesn't create a good impression. And as a special education teacher, you are often under extra scrutiny, as some people still think you are not very busy because you work with a limited number of students.

Ask for Help, Offer to Help

To have a friend, you have to be one—this adage certainly applies to you as a special education teacher, and abiding by this saying can have some positive results for you. Look below to see how reaching out to colleagues can reap benefits for you—and your students.

▶ 1. If you are a new teacher, you probably have many questions and requests for your more experienced colleagues and wonder what you could possibly have to offer them. As a special education teacher, there are many ways you can repay your general education colleagues for their help. This kind of give-and-take is a very important way for you to gain credibility and goodwill in your school— something that can benefit both you and your students.

▶ 2. During the first few weeks of school, you will probably be able to identify those people in your school who are friendly and willing to help. Most teachers who extend a helping hand do so because they remember what it was like to be new and to feel alone. Don't hesitate to approach them, but when you do so remember your manners. Arrange to meet at a time convenient for them, get to the point, and say thank you.

▶ 3. At some point, you may feel you would like to reciprocate their kindness. Here are some ideas to consider.
   a. Share some useful activity books, project ideas, or academic games.
   b. Use your own expertise as a special education teacher. Offer to include one or more students from the general education classroom in your groups if there are some who could benefit.
   c. Provide some adaptation ideas that may be helpful for some of the aforementioned students. But do so in a sensitive way. Don't assume your colleague is unable to adapt work or has never done so.
   d. Be available when possible to assist on field trips for classes in which your students with disabilities are included. If you have a self-contained classroom, ask if your students can be included if you and an adequate number of helpers accompany them.
   e. Share materials; offer to substitute for a duty; buy your colleague his or her favorite candy bar, soda, or snack.

▶ 4. You'll be surprised at the goodwill you can create and the respect you will gain for yourself if you accept kindness from others and repay them. An added benefit is that your students will gain also. Teachers who respect you as a professional may be more willing to work with your students, and this is perhaps the best outcome of your efforts.

Other Supports for New Teachers

Most districts have avenues of support for new teachers outside of their schools. Find out what they are, and take advantage of them. These may differ slightly from district to district, but they are there. So be sure to check out what your school system has to offer.

▶ 1. Your district should have workshops and other educational opportunities to offer—and sometimes these are free. Usually, a number of these are geared for special education teachers. But don't hesitate to attend workshops that may be earmarked for regular education teachers such as those dealing with curriculum development in specific subject areas. After all, your goal should be to see that your students are able to access the general education curriculum as much as possible—so it's your job to be up to date on the latest subject matter and methods of teaching. Buddy teachers, other special education teachers, or your principal or special education administrator should be able to help you access these opportunities.

▶ 2. Most school districts have teachers' unions that will provide help for you if you feel you are having problems in your school situation that are not being addressed by your principal or other administrative staff to whom you report. Within your school, you should also have a staff member who is your union representative and who may be able to answer some questions for you and should be able to direct you to someone in the union who can be of assistance. Certainly use these resources if you feel it necessary, but do make every effort to work with those within your school to address your problem(s) before seeking outside assistance. Most people outside your school to whom you go for help will want to know what you have done to address the problem within the chain of command in your own school.

▶ 3. As a special education teacher, you should have a special education department in your district with a support staff available to you. This department may offer workshops or inservices also. Find out how you can get on their mailing list so you will know about offerings that may be of interest. The support staff might be available to come out to your school to discuss concerns about your students or suggest academic and behavioral strategies that you could use.

▶ 4. There may be a technology department in your district that includes assistive technology for students with special education needs. They might offer inservices or workshops also and may have a variety of equipment and materials they loan out to teachers. Be sure to find out how to access this department in your district and learn about what they can provide.

■ Suggested Readings

Bender, W. (2002). *Differentiating instruction for students with learning disabilities.* Thousand Oaks, CA: Corwin.

> This book provides varied instructional techniques and modifications for inclusive and individual classes. Many ideas and examples are included.

Fister, S., & Kemp, K. (1995). *TGIF: But what will I do on Monday?* Longmont, CO: Sopris West.

> This collection of practical accommodations meets the needs of all students who present challenges to instruction.

Fister, S., & Kemp, K. (1995). *TGIF: Making it work on Monday.* Longmont, CO: Sopris West.

> Filled with 200 reproducibles, this book is a companion to *TGIF: But What Will I Do on Monday?*

Franklin Smutny, J., & von Fremd, S. E. (2004). *Differentiating for the young child: Teaching strategies across the content area (K–3).* Thousand Oaks, CA: Corwin.

> Teachers of young students can find help in identifying differences and adjusting lessons based on their needs in content areas including language arts, social studies, science, and math.

Holzschuher, C. (1997). *How to manage your inclusive classroom.* Huntington Beach, CA: Teacher Created Materials.

> This practical book provides many samples and examples of making adaptations for a variety of academic areas. It also includes practical ideas on cooperative learning, assessments and evaluations, and communicating with parents, and an annotated list of children's literature that includes characters with disabilities.

Jensen, W. R., Rhode, G., & Reavis, H. (1994). *The tough kid toolbox.* Longmont, CO: Sopris West.

> This book supplements *The Tough Kid Book* with additional strategies and more in-depth explanations. Most helpful are the many reproducibles that accompany the strategies included here as well as those found in *The Tough Kid Book.*

McConnell, F. K., & Gilliam, J. (2000). *New teacher's survival guide.* Longmont, CO: Sopris West.

> This is a how-to book for establishing and maintaining a positive classroom climate, and it also provides ideas for effective classroom management and instruction.

Pierangelo, R. (1994). *A survival kit for the special education teacher.* West Nyack, NY: The Center for Applied Research in Education.

This book contains many reproducible forms, checklists, and sample letters as well as guidelines for evaluation, remediation, classroom management, testing modifications, IEP development, and more.

Rathvon, N. (1999). *Effective school interventions.* New York: Guilford Press.

Research-based interventions for academic achievement and social competence are included in this useful book. The interventions can be used for classrooms, small groups, and individual students. Modifications are included.

Reif, S., & Heimburge, J. (1996). *How to reach and teach all students in the inclusive classroom: Ready-to-use strategies, lessons and activities for teaching students with diverse learning needs.* West Nyack, NY: The Center for Applied Research in Education.

This very useful book contains many ready-to-use strategies, lessons, and activities for students with diverse learning styles, ability levels, and behaviors that can be found in inclusive classrooms today.

Rhode, G., Jenson, W., & Reavis, H. (1992). *The tough kid book.* Longmont, CO: Sopris West.

This very practical book bypasses idealistic suggestions for dealing with difficult students and offers insight into a variety of inappropriate student behaviors. It provides a variety of workable and effective strategies to try that are useful at all grade levels. Many reproducibles are included.

Salend, S. J. (2001). *Creating inclusive classrooms: Effective and reflective practices* (Rev. 4th ed.). Upper Saddle River, NJ: Prentice Hall.

This very thorough book covers a broad range of special education subjects including understanding the diverse educational needs of students with disabilities, differentiating instruction in academic areas, creating collaborative relationships, and fostering communication. Useful Web sites are listed throughout, and a compact disc titled "Developing Quality IEPs: A Case-Base Tutorial" is included.

Sprick, R., Garrison, M., & Howard, L. (1998). *CHAMPS.* Longmont, CO: Sopris West.

Many useful proactive and positive approaches to classroom management and for dealing with a variety of inappropriate behaviors can be found in this book. Some reproducibles are included.

■ References

DuFour, R. (2004). What is a professional learning community? *Educational Leadership, 61*(8), 6–11.

Vasa, S. F. (1981). Alternative procedures for grading handicapped students in the secondary schools. *Education Unlimited, 3*(1), 16–23.

Ysseldyke, J. E., Algozzine, B., & Thurlow, M. L. (2000). *Critical issues in special education* (3rd ed.). Boston: Houghton Mifflin.

Web Sites

Cooperative Educational Service Agency: http://www.cesa7.k12.wi.us/sped
Link: Dept. & Services, then Special Education
Milwaukee Public Schools: http://www.milwaukeepublicschools.org
Link: Parents, then Special Education
National Association of School Psychologists: http://nasponline.org
Link: Accessible Index, then Public Policy link to IDEA information, then OSERS (Office of Special Education and Rehabilitative Services) IDEA 2004 Policy Briefs on Major Topics, then IEP
State of Wisconsin Department of Public Instruction: http://www.dpi.state.wi.us
Link: For Parents, then Special Education, then Index of Topics, then Individualized Education Program
Wrightslaw: http://www.wrightslaw.com
Link: IDEA 2004, then What you need to know about IEP

■ Index